T0339523

"This guide provides CEOs, future CEOs, managers, and aspiring team leaders with a practical tool to accelerate performance, drive talent engagement and generate greater results."

Chantal Riopel, *General Manager, Marriott*

"The authors wrote a must-have book to help leaders become better leaders. It's the kind of guide that you want to have and refer to when you are looking for solutions to build strong leadership as well as collaborative and learning cultures."

Xavier Tedeschi, *Director of Human Relations, Innothera*

"This book is exceptional. It is the most comprehensive explanation of the principles, methods, and tools of a new approach to the development of individual and team leadership that involves organizational co-creation, collaboration and learning from and with others."

Yury Boshyk, *Author; CEO, Founder of Global Executive Learning, and Business Driven Action Learning*

"This comprehensive guide presents much needed scientific research findings on the impact of Codevelopment Action Learning for organizations across all sectors. It is a significant contribution to our field and will help practitioners to better implement Action Learning and obtain more sustainable results."

Heidi Schaefer, *International Foundation for Action Learning Co-Director (2016 to 2022) and Action Learning Practitioner at Action Learning Centre (ALC) Limited*

"This inspiring book outlines the pathway to build more co-leadership and creativity in today's environment. A must-read to build a collaborative culture and the leadership capabilities of tomorrow."

Annie Desautels, *Vice-President, Accès Desjardins*

"This is an important and uplifting book offering a whole new way to rethink ways of working together. As a strong promoter of cross-functional collaboration, I found in this book an innovative solution to talent mobilization, employee retention and innovation development."

Benoit Desgroseillers, *Vice-President, Talent Development, Finance Montreal*

"This book is a fantastic resource about how-tos of building and growing cohesive teams. Having been myself a leader in large corporations for many years, I understand how this book is a critical read for all leaders aiming to increase collaboration with their teams, and help break down the silos of their organization."

Hélène Blanchette, *Founder & CEO, BizAndGive LLC*

"I highly recommend this book to all heads of NGO and non-profit organizations that are looking for ways to stimulate collaboration and co-learning. We have used Codevelopment Action Learning to accelerate the integration of immigrant women. Since then, internally, we regularly use this approach to accelerate our projects and it has significantly improved our team cohesion and effectiveness."

Régine Alende Tshombokongo, *General Director of Centre d'encadrement pour jeunes femmes immigrantes/CEJFI (Center for Young immigrants Women)*

"This is a much-needed book that inspires you to build a better future. You will find an effective approach to bring leaders together to grow and learn from each other for better results. Try it, and you will be amazed by the power of Codevelopment Action Learning described in this guide."

Phil Lenir, *President, CoachingOurselves International Inc.*

"We are proud to be part of the success stories related in this book. Codevelopment Action Learning groups are an integral component of our Learning & Development strategy for Leaders at all levels. Our goal is to promote cross-collaboration and sharing of practices between managers of different areas with these effective and inspiring learning spaces. This approach has helped us build our leadership community by enabling leaders to grow and learn from each other."

Sylvain Proulx, *Learning and Development Leader, UQAM (University of Quebec in Montreal)*

"Codevelopment Action Learning groups enabled us to accelerate leadership development and develop a shared management culture. Over the years, these groups have become more than just a cornerstone of our learning activities; they have become a key motivational tool and a benchmark for interdepartmental collaboration for both managers and employees."

Marc-André Vigeant, *Human Resources Senior Director, City of Laval*

"Co-create, Accelerate and Grow is a must-have book to implement Codevelopment Action Learning to support entrepreneurs build stronger businesses and partnerships. We finally found a way to accelerate entrepreneurship!"

David Chapman, *President, GROW-studio*

"The work environment is undergoing major changes. We have here a wonderful book to guide any leader with an innovative approach to co-create solutions and stimulate cross-collaboration for new possibilities."

Chantal Lamoureux, *President, IQPF (Institut québécois de planification financière)*

This book is the perfect demonstration of how business and academia can come together to innovate. The authors teach you the Codevelopment Action Learning approach through concrete practical cases, combined with scientific data that confirms how this approach can stimulate cross-collaboration among leaders and enable them to become more effective by learning from each other.

Dr. Danielle Laberge, *Interim Rector of the Université du Québec à Montréal (UQAM). Also served as Provost (Academic), Executive Provost and is Professor of Sociology at UQAM (University of Quebec in Montreal)*

"I recommend this inspiring book to all leaders of organizations that work in the field of entrepreneurship and economic development. The Codevelopment Action-Learning Approach is a creative way to learn from each other and quickly gain new insights to improve business practices as a start-up or as a new entrepreneur!"

Véronique Perreault, *Innovation Advisor, DEL (Développement économique de l'agglomération de Longueuil)*

"This book will get you to think and inspire you to act. After testing Codevelopment Action-Learning, I was fascinated by this strong people-centered approach that brings people together through diversity of thought. It stimulates interdisciplinary perspectives that promotes creativity and innovation so that people and organizations can achieve their goals."

Pierre Lainey, *Full-time Lecturer-HEC-Montréal, Fellow C.M.C, Author in the fields of Leadership and Management*

Codevelopment Action Learning for Business

Workplaces where the focus is on innovation, teamwork and learning have become a reality, thanks to a simple, practical, and effective approach called CAL: Codevelopment Action Learning. This book will help you to create a collaborative and empowering culture in your organization.

The CAL method, tools, and theoretical foundations for each component are presented in detail here. Real case studies and research findings on the tangible benefits and impacts of the approach enrich its content. Authored by a dynamic team of CAL business coaches and academics, the knowledge is shared in a straightforward and accessible manner.

Business leaders, entrepreneurs, human resources and learning professionals, coaches, facilitators, scholar practitioners, and more will welcome this book's thought-provoking guidance to co-create solutions, accelerate goals, and grow capabilities for the 21st century.

Maxime Paquet, PhD, is an I/O psychologist, expert in workplace evaluation and training programs through a variety of in-person and online methods, including Codevelopment Action Learning (CAL). Since 2013, together with Nathalie Lafranchise, he has been leading an action-research program named Codev-Action, focusing on the optimization and outcomes of CAL groups.

Nathalie Sabourin, MSc, CHRP, co-founder of The Co-Leadership Group, is an experienced strengths-based coach, entrepreneur, and author, who unites teams and empowers leaders. She implemented CAL in diverse businesses to accelerate potential, innovation, and learning. Nathalie inspires and shares her expertise on co-leadership, cross-collaboration, and action learning through client engagements, podcasts, articles, and university engagements.

Nathalie Lafranchise, PhD, focuses her research on professional support, specifically: CAL, mentoring, skills development, interpersonal and group communication, as well as emotional intelligence and competence. Since 2013, together with Maxime Paquet, she has been leading an action-research program named Codev-Action, focusing on the optimization and outcomes of CAL groups.

Ron Cheshire, MBA, PCC, is a strengths-based Leadership Coach with 25+ years of senior business executive experience. Certified by ICF, Gallup, and Erickson International, he excels in fostering growth by harnessing individuals' unique strengths. With a passion for coaching and CAL facilitation, Ron leaves a lasting impact on individuals and teams in organizations.

Codevelopment Action Learning for Business

Co-create. Accelerate. Grow

Maxime Paquet

Nathalie Sabourin

Nathalie Lafranchise and

Ron Cheshire

Routledge
Taylor & Francis Group

NEW YORK AND LONDON

Designed cover image: © Getty images

First published 2024
by Routledge
605 Third Avenue, New York, NY 10158

and by Routledge
4 Park Square, Milton Park, Abingdon, Oxon, OX14 4RN

Routledge is an imprint of the Taylor & Francis Group, an informa business

© 2024 Maxime Paquet, Nathalie Sabourin, Nathalie Lafranchise, and Ron Cheshire

ISBN: 9781032625676 (hbk)
ISBN: 9781032625607 (pbk)
ISBN: 9781032625720 (ebk)

DOI: 10.4324/9781032625720

Typeset in Times new Roman
by codeMantra

Contents

About the authors

Maxime Paquet, PhD, Industrial and Organizational (I/O) Psychologist, Associate professor, Department of Psychology, University of Montreal; maxime.paquet.8@umontreal.ca

His work as an I/O psychologist in the Quebec healthcare network has made him an expert at evaluating many aspects of organizational development, such as improving workplace climate and employee recognition, and has helped him develop support and training programs through a variety of in-person and online methods, including Codevelopment Action Learning (CAL). Since 2008, he has been a CAL facilitator, trainer and supported hundreds of organizations wishing to implement the approach.

Since 2013, together with Nathalie Lafranchise, he has been leading an action-research program named Codev-Action, which includes three projects funded by the Social Sciences and Humanities Research Council of Canada (SSHRC) and focusing on the optimization and outcomes of CAL groups for a variety of populations across all sectors.

Nathalie Sabourin, MSc, CHRP. Co-Founder – The Co-Leadership Group (Montreal, Canada); www.coleadershipgroup.com; nsabourin@coleadershipgroup.com

Nathalie is an experienced strengths-based coach, author, and dynamic entrepreneur who unites teams and empowers leaders to reach new heights, together. She partners with her clients from various businesses to accelerate their objectives with highly collaborative coaching journeys. She has successfully implemented CAL in diverse organizations and trained hundreds of internal and external facilitators to accelerate teamwork, innovation, and learning – the essential capabilities for the future.

In addition, Nathalie has contributed her coaching insights to three CAL action-research projects, has co-authored two practical guides to implement CAL in businesses, and written several articles on co-leadership. She has also designed creative resources and tools including the recognized *CoachingOurselves "FlashCodev" guide* to stimulate teamwork, engagement, and a learning culture.

She inspires and shares her expertise on co-leadership, cross-collaboration, and action learning through podcasts, conferences, articles, and university engagements. She is a Gallup CliftonStrengths Coach (since 2008) as well as a *CoachingOurselves* and *e2Grow* partner, with a passion to discover the world with her family.

Nathalie Lafranchise, PhD, Full Professor, Department of social and public communications, Université du Québec à Montreal (UQAM); lafranchise.nathalie@uqam.ca

Nathalie is responsible for the Graduate Mentoring Program at UQAM's Faculty of Communication. She is also an undergraduate internship supervisor in Human and Organizational Communication. Her research focuses on professional support, specifically: CAL groups; mentoring; skills development support; co-construction of knowledge; interpersonal and group communication; as well as emotional communication, regulation, intelligence, and competence.

Since 2013, together with Maxime Paquet, she has been leading an action-research program named Codev-Action, which includes three projects funded by the SSHRC and focusing on the optimization and outcomes of CAL groups for a variety of populations across all sectors.

Ron Cheshire, MBA, PCC. Co-Founder – The Co-Leadership Group (Montreal, Canada); www.coleadershipgroup.com; rcheshire@coleadershipgroup.com

Ron Cheshire is a strengths-based Leadership Coach with more than 25 years' expertise as a senior leader in business development, investment management, team leadership, and partnerships. His passion lies in nurturing leaders and teams, providing individual and team coaching across various levels, from managers to high potential leaders and business executives. Ron empowers his clients to embrace their roles confidently, envision the future, set impactful goals, and lead with a strengths-based positive mindset.

As an accomplished Gallup Certified Strengths Coach (Clifton-Strengths), Erickson Certified Professional Coach, and Professional Certified Coach (PCC) with ICF, he is also an experienced facilitator of CAL groups. Ron's people-centric approach centres on rediscovering and harnessing individuals' unique strengths and untapped potential. Beyond his professional endeavours, he remains fervently dedicated to soccer and skiing. Concordia University (EMBA) and Carleton University (BA, Economics) have equipped Ron with the educational foundation to drive success in his multifaceted career.

Contributors

Translation and proofreading – Diana Halfpenny

Graphic design – Karole Landry

Mentorship and guidance – Yury Boshyk

Advisory panel – Catherine Bédard, Louis Bélisle, Pierre Lainey, Josiane Parnet, and Eve Zeville

Foreword

This book is exceptional. It is the most comprehensive explanation of the principles, methods, and tools of a new approach to the development of individual and team leadership that involves organizational co-creation, the active assistance and collaboration from and with others.

The authors discuss the principles, methods, and the "how" of Codevelopment Action Learning (CAL) in a very practical, meticulous, and structured way. Numerous real-world examples are included, as are many very useful tools and templates. The book also provides a simple, yet novel, peer-reviewed, and precise way to measure these outcomes—important for those who wish to see factual proof of the approach's results for individuals, teams, companies, and organizations. The book will help businesses and leaders make a major step-change in accelerating growth by enhancing measurable behavioural change through greater leadership self-awareness and systematic intentional problem-solving for individuals and teams. The method is already being used by leaders of businesses large and small to clarify growth opportunities and solve challenges, mainly at management and board levels. For executive teams, it is used for discussing and defining business strategies and dealing with succession and a host of other issues. And for leadership and organizational development professionals, it will also change their mind and approach about how to help further develop leadership skills for people in their organization.

The "learning" part of CAL is very much part of the approach, and it aligns with the most recent practices and insights that indicate that learning is the most important driver of other success factors in all companies, in all business sectors, and in all industries. Even in Silicon Valley and in other creative business hubs in the world, start-ups and established companies use the following mantra to describe this reality and process as "build, test, learn"—to be repeated as long as it takes until you get your product or service right—preferably, as one author recently wrote, by "learning at the speed of light."

This "learning" is clearly tied to action and CAL has also provided a new dimension to the Action Learning practitioner's understanding of the phrase, "no action without learning, no learning without action." This is done by a greater emphasis on key matters such as accountability to business sponsors through measurable results and greater sharing of personal development goals among participants.

The authors' approach, referred to as "Codevelopment Action Learning" or (CAL) is not to be confused with "Critical Action Learning," a quite different approach, nor with "Codevelopment" per se, a practice used in the French-speaking world in the 1990s and still today that had a mission to "create an environment, method and process that permits an individual to immerse themselves and to think actively about their job together with other colleagues, evolving their own models of action." This book's understanding of Codevelopment is new and more precise and has been developed by a new generation (the authors) who, while honouring the contributions of the original founders and practices, felt it was time to change and add some essential principles and practices. This group came together as a core team as two very experienced consultants, Nathalie Sabourin and Ron Cheshire, with two well-known university professors, Nathalie Lafranchise and Maxime Paquet, to make some major changes to Codevelopment's method. They pay tribute to Adrien Payette and Claude Champagne from Quebec, Canada, as the "co-creators" of Codevelopment but the authors and other collaborators went beyond the "legacy" 1990s model of Codevelopment and the way it was and is generally practiced in France and the Francophone countries.

The "new generation" authors began working together in 2013 introducing more accountability, accelerating learning from each other, and deepening the process of change for Codevelopment. In essence, the new team wanted to be more open and flexible, regarding traditional legacy practices and principles. They were also passionate about bringing their new model to the English-speaking world—and hence this book. This is the first-English-language handbook about CAL and is a fundamental revision of Codevelopment practice used in the Francophone world until very recently.

CAL thus incorporates a robust and accountable structure for participants ("less discussion and more action"), enhances facilitation and coaching in its work, and certainly provides a clear and peer-reviewed return on expectation (ROE) measurement with evidence of progress. Fundamental was their incorporation of new insights from their own and international research and experiences. The toolkit section in the book is a superb example of CAL's ethos and practice with its blend of thoughtfulness and concern for continuous personal growth for leaders.

It is perhaps helpful to explain the "Action Learning" context of CAL. The use of Action Learning has now become widespread in the business world since its founding in the early 1970s in the U.K. by Reg. W. Revans, a Cambridge scientist turned educational reformer and consultant. It is a values-based and experiential way to educate and develop people and organizations with clearly defined approaches to process and objectives. Action Learning is having a significant impact in the business community. In my research, I have identified 65 different varieties (at last count) of which nine and now ten can be referred to as mainstream, that are being used by major businesses and industries throughout the world. CAL has certainly joined the ranks of this special group and it will be even more impactful as it becomes more widely known in the English-speaking world. Already, CAL has gained widespread praise from business leaders, Organization and Leadership Development practitioners, participants, and academic circles alike.

In the world of experiential and Action Learning practitioners, CAL has gained traction because of its structured, yet collaborative, measurable, and very practical approach, including that it allows for participants to make thoughtful suggestions to problems and opportunities to other participants based on their past and present experiences.

The CAL learning method emphasizes that learning and sharing includes the use of intentional reflection because otherwise "experience is just repetition" of the same. Plato, once commented that experience helped develop the best but also the worst flute players in Athens. Reflecting on and learning from one's experience and then doing things differently is the essence of success.

CAL participants learn with others in small groups, sometimes from different organizations and roles, providing them with greater insight into their own dilemma or issue. All engaged in the CAL process consciously learn together, including the facilitators and participants. CAL is also focused on maximizing the benefits to a business, including developing an intact team within an organization and accelerating an individual leader's development.

Action Learning arose during the 1970s and 1980s–turbulent times for the world and business. In 2023, the world looks even more turbulent with authors like Roubini, the economics professor who was one of the few who predicted the economic crash of 2007–2008, and now warning us of "megathreats." But he also writes, that along with global leaders, that there is still time to fix our problems through active collaboration and concerted effort. It is my view, that in this critical period for humanity, CAL and Action Learning will play a crucial role in helping companies and leaders align with common objectives and a greater purpose for the survival and flourishing of humanity—the very nature of Action Learning's and CAL's values.

Before his passing, Warren Bennis, one of the most influential thought leaders of learning and leadership development, advised business leaders when asked "What is the most important thing that leaders today need to know in order to be successful?" He replied, "Leaders today need to understand action-learning (stet) and how to apply this unique form of learning in a team setting…".

Action Learning and CAL are clearly headed to be of great service to us all.

Dr. Yury Boshyk
CEO and Founder of Global Executive Learning, Chairman and Founder of the annual Global Forum on Strategic Transformations,

Leadership and Learning, former Professor at the International Institute for Management Development (IMD) in Switzerland, and founder of Business Driven Action Learning.

Author of various books about Action Learning, including Business driven Action Learning: Global best practices (2000) and Action Learning worldwide: Experiences of leadership and organizational development (2002).

Acknowledgements

Over the past few years, the Codevelopment Action Learning (CAL) approach has been implemented more and more, all around the world. Facilitators have been trained and coached and thousands of CAL groups have been set up in every sector and in many different countries. As proof or this, three important university-partnered research projects have been conducted in Canada, where the method originated, to measure CAL's impact and look for ways to improve it. This book is the fruit of a joint venture between the authors who have variously practiced the approach and worked as university researchers for the past ten years.

We'd like to thank all our partners, clients, colleagues, and friends who have encouraged us to share our experiences. We're finally fulfilling our dream of bringing CAL to the English-speaking world by publishing a book that presents the pragmatic, practical side of the approach and also supports it with empirical research data.

We wish to express our special thanks to Dr. Yury Boshyk, CEO, Global Executive Learning (GEL), who has believed in us from the outset and has always encouraged us to share our thoughts and research results. His support has been a constant source of encouragement, even during the major challenges to the project brought about by the COVID-19 pandemic. Thank you for providing us the unique opportunity to bring CAL to the 2023 Global Forum on Leadership, Learning and Strategic Change, held in Barcelona.

We share our gratitude to Meredith Norwich, our editor at Routledge, who accepted to partner with us to launch CAL to the world with this book. Your positive energy, trust, and focus made a difference for us.

We also wish to acknowledge the contributions and support of our advisory panel, consisting of Catherine Bédard, Louis Bélisle, Pierre Lainey, Josiane Parnet, and Eve Zeville, who gave us the motivation we needed to reach the finish line.

Our thanks to all of you who worked with us on our various projects. These partnerships enabled us to expand our vision of CAL and combine it with aspects of other methods, such as appreciative and positive approaches to learning.

We would also like to thank the AQCP (*Association québécoise du codéveloppement professionnel*) with whom we've worked for several years now to implement CAL training sessions. Thanks also to the IFAL

(International Foundation for Action Learning) Executive Committee members who were the first to allow us to present CAL during a series of webinars on the different forms of Action Learning.

A special thanks to collaborators Diana Halfpenny and Karole Landry for their creative contributions to the book. Diana, you worked hard to transfer our thoughts and ideas into English: your work does more than make our ideas comprehensible to an English-speaking readership, it makes them a pleasure to read! Karole, you also worked hard to transfer our words into inspiring images that shows what CAL is all about.

Finally, we would also like to acknowledge the invaluable contribution of the method's co-creators, Adrien Payette and Claude Champagne. Without their work, ours wouldn't have been possible.

We hope this book will inspire you to implement CAL in order to generate new perspectives, to work together to creatively solve today's challenges as well as tomorrow's and, above all, to learn from each other.

Many thanks!

Maxime, Nathalie, Nathalie, and Ron

Personal thanks

In closing, we'd like to thank our families, friends, and members of our professional network for their support throughout this project.

From Maxime Paquet

Nathalie L., without you, I wouldn't have embarked on this CAL adventure or on any of our other exciting projects. Your love, your presence, and your guiding hand are a source of constant support and creativity, self-discipline, and strength. Thank you, quite simply, for being at my side and for who you are.

To Nathalie S., thanks for your unfailing strength, your drive, your ideas, and for the fun we had working together, and to Ron, for your wisdom, patience, guidance, and reassurance.

Without the three of you, this unique blend of all our strengths would never have seen the light of day.

Thank you to everyone with whom I've had the opportunity to practice CAL, who have sustained my passion for the approach, and helped me develop as a CAL practitioner and researcher.

Finally, I'd like to acknowledge all the students with whom I've worked. Thank you for giving me a reason to keep on doing what I do and to believe in building the skills of the future.

From Nathalie Sabourin

First of all, I share my love and gratitude to my amazing husband Ron, who has always inspired me to dream big. You've always been my partner in everything I do. I'm so proud to have co-authored this book with you to promote co-leadership in businesses and build a better future. I would also like to thank my two gorgeous children, Benoit and Geneviève, for their open hearts. You are the very definition of the words "Being happy, together." I love you both deeply.

This new book is also a tribute to my grandfather, Rolland P. Sabourin, who pioneered the role of "Farming community facilitator" that laid the foundation for agricultural cooperation in Quebec, still fully alive today. I now understand the roots of my passion for CAL.

Thank you to my parents Agathe and Louis. Your desire for knowledge, your inspiration to excel, and your generosity have fuelled all my dreams and projects. Thank you so much, *maman*, for coming to Paris for my first major CAL conference and reviewing my first book in French!

I would like to thank Nathalie L. for the partnership we have, that's a true example of what can be achieved by combining our strengths and working as friends for over a decade. Also, a special thank you to Maxime. Through our many meetings and brainstorming sessions, always enlivened by your positive outlook, openness, and curiosity, together we were able to make our dreamed-of book a reality.

Finally, a sincere thank you to all my clients, partners, and The Co-Leadership Group Team, who dared to experiment CAL in various contexts to make a real difference, together, and most of all, who supported the creation of this book. All my gratitude to my dear friends who gave me wings and inspired me throughout my journey.

From Nathalie Lafranchise

First, I'd like to thank my life partner, research partner, and co-author, Maxime. While our relationship has been great for both our careers, its greatest impact has been on my personal life. Through your endless thirst for knowledge, you're my anchor, my strength, and a source of inspiration.

Thanks to Renée Houde, my mentor and now my friend. You helped give birth to my career. Without you, I probably wouldn't be where I am today. Thank you for believing in me. Your kindness, support, and discipline are exemplary.

I'd like to thank my parents, Micheline and Réjean, who placed such a high value on education; it's a value I'll always carry with me. They've always been an example to me of mutual support, sharing, commitment, and respect for others. Without knowing it, they embody and have passed on to me the principles of CAL, which I do my best to pass on in turn.

I thank my daughter, Mélodie, who has to share her mother with her many university commitments: I want you to know that you have always inspired and motivated me. Now a wonderful young woman, your sense of responsibility, your professional attitude, and your drive to excel makes you shine in your chosen profession. These are all core CAL values that I dare to hope I've nurtured in you.

My thanks to Louise Lafortune for having taught me the values of peer support and for having been such a great role model in leading an academic team and managing large-scale projects.

A big thank you to the students who took part in my many research projects as well as to all those whom I taught. It's a privilege to have the opportunity to help you pursue your academic and professional goals.

Finally, thank you to my co-authors, Nathalie S. and Ron, for working with me and providing us with this unique opportunity to share CAL with others outside the French-speaking world.

From Ron Cheshire

First, I'd like to share my deepest gratitude for my wife and co-author, Nathalie S., my partner at every stage of my career and life journey. I'm proud that we can pursue our shared passion for CAL and co-leadership together while building our amazing family. Every day, I'm inspired by our work to help leaders and teams innovate and thrive with transformational and shared leadership.

I thank our children, Benoit and Geneviève, from the bottom of my heart for all the great dinner table conversations we've had, and the many wonderful trips we've taken to fun destinations, that have helped us grow, together. This book is for you, so you keep on learning and being curious and open to others.

My thanks also to my sister, Liisa, Agathe, Louis, my friends, and my clients, who believed I could successfully transition from the financial sector to becoming a coach for teams, groups, and leaders. I hope reading this book will be a source of inspiration for you.

Finally, I would like to acknowledge the unique contribution of my co-authors, Maxime and Nathalie L., for contributing their in-depth research on the impacts of the CAL to the book. Most of all, I would like to thank them for being my mentors for CAL and for their shared commitment to creating a better world.

Introduction

Co-create. Accelerate. Grow

Imagine a workplace where:

- silos are replaced by co-creation and collaboration;
- instead of problems, people work on creative solutions;
- the culture focuses less on mistakes, and more on learning from each other.

What do you think when you read those words? Are they inspiring, or unrealistic?

In fact, those scenarios aren't just feasible, they've actually happening! Recently, with a simple, practical, and effective approach. And, we're writing this book because we want to share what we've learned from that experience of over 15 years, with thousands of participants from the private and public sectors.

Today's businesses are forced to rapidly adapt to a variety of economic, technological, social, environmental, and now health-related changes, all happening at the same time. The speed at which these changes occur means we must constantly be ready to innovate in order to stay competitive. This means businesses, leaders, and teams must be creative and ready to learn, unlearn, and relearn, continuously and together.

A new way of working together and engaging with others is urgently needed.

To stand out and ensure they can survive in today's challenging business world, organizations must create stimulating work environments that foster creativity, teamwork, trust, and continuous learning. These environments give their employees the courage to act and take risks in order to implement new ways of doing things.

In fact, this new world calls for new capabilities, such as learning how to use artificial intelligence and the social media platforms that enable us to process information. However, at almost one quarter of the way through the 21st century, technology still serves us, albeit differently than in the industrial age, but it still has limits; it can't do everything for us.

DOI: 10.4324/9781032625720-1

After spending so many years on technological development, we're now realizing that, increasingly, the capabilities of the future are based on human skills, collaborative leadership as well as the ability to innovate and continuously learn and grow.[1]

We need creative ways to respond to our current organizational and business challenges: ways that, by sharing our experiences, take us out of our comfort zones, bring us together, and help us develop new insights. Ways that will help us create learning and empowering cultures and assist people in reaching their full potential.

What's different about this book?

We are writing this book to share a simple, practical, and effective method to **co-create** solutions, **accelerate** goals, and **grow** capabilities for the 21st century.

The approach is called Codeveloppement Action Learning (CAL). It's an approach where participants who are ready to learn from one another are formed into groups. The approach includes an effective, straightforward, and proven method that's easy to implement. Over the next few weeks or months, the groups meet in order to co-create solutions to sometimes challenging work and real-life situations the participants have shared with one another. They will apply these solutions to their work and use the process to boost their creativity and collaboration, accelerate their goals, and grow to their full potential.

The book you're currently reading is a practical guide that presents all the steps involved in CAL, explains how to facilitate it in a group, and how to implement such a group in an organization.

What we're sharing with you here is the fruit of 15 years' experience and knowledge based on implementing CAL in countless organizations and teams and supported by ten years of action research.

In other words, the method described in this book is effective, straightforward, and proven, as illustrated by several real-life organization and business results.

For readers interested in learning about the origins of CAL, at various points in Parts 1 and 2, we've included a section explaining the theoretical basis of each step and its component parts. Without losing sight of the book's primarily practical focus, the goal of these sections is to provide opportunities for more in-depth thinking and suggestions for further reading.

The book is divided into four parts:

- **Part 1 – Codevelopment Action Learning groups.** This part summarizes the goals and main benefits of the CAL approach (Chapter 1), outlines how it works, and lists the five underlying principles (Chapter 2).
- **Part 2 – The Codevelopment Action Learning method.** This part introduces the CAL method and the role of a CAL group.

In Chapters 3 to 11, you experience each of the steps first-hand by reading about the story of Emilio, a team leader who uses CAL to develop his leadership skills. Then, each of the steps is broken down into its objectives, benefits, and how it can be facilitated. Finally, for scholar practitioners, we present the theories that inspired each step and that explain why it works.

- **Part 3 – Is Your Organization Ready for CAL?** This part presents the winning conditions for successfully implementing and sustaining CAL groups (Chapter 12) and illustrates them through real-life examples of different organizations that have benefited from CAL (Chapters 14 and 15). Since facilitation is a crucial aspect of a CAL group's effectiveness, the selection and training of CAL facilitators is covered in Chapter 13.
- **Part 4 – The Outcomes of Codevelopment Action Learning.** The final section goes into more depth on CAL's impacts and benefits. After outlining the potential benefits (Chapter 16), the next two chapters discuss the practical benefits, through real-life examples of groups operating in such areas as the public sector (health, higher education), the private sector (entrepreneurs, professional associations), and the non-profit sector. Chapter 19 presents the results of research measuring CAL's impact. These metrics can help you build your business case and help convince decision-makers to implement CAL in your business.

Who should read this book?

Decision-makers

CAL is a good choice for groups of leaders and managers, experts, professionals, and teams. If your strategic priorities focus on innovation, collaboration, trust, developing teams, talents, and communities of leaders, or if you want to find a way to accelerate projects and/or objectives, you might want to give CAL a try. The advantages of this method are that it's inexpensive and delivers real, rapid results.

The support that CAL provides can also make a significant difference in retaining hard-to-recruit employees.

If you want to zero in on the most relevant parts for you, Part 1 summarizes CAL's effectiveness and outcomes and Part 4 discusses the benefits in greater depth, to help you decide if CAL is the right choice for you.

HRD and leadership and development managers

Are you tasked with creating a culture of learning and collaboration? Are you looking for ways to develop soft skills that require time and practice to build? Do you want to implement CAL in such a way that it generates effective, long-lasting results?

In that case, start with Part 1, but then move on to Part 3, where you'll learn how to successfully start, run, and sustain a CAL group. If some of your stakeholders are still on the fence, Part 4 will give you some much-needed metrics to flesh out your business case. This is also where you can pick up some ideas for recording the results of your CAL group, as it may be your job to do so.

Consultants, trainers, coaches, and facilitators

You're probably familiar with traditional action learning, group coaching, and other peer-based learning methods. If so, you already have the knowledge and skills required to facilitate CAL and integrate it into your practice. But regardless of your previous experience in this field, we recommend you start by learning about the CAL approach.

After reviewing Part 1, the part that will be most useful to you is Part 2, which takes you step by step through the method. Chapter 14 also has some useful tips for your own journey as a CAL facilitator.

Scholar practitioners and academics

If you were included in one of the previous three categories, and you're also interested in the theoretical and practical basis of the methods you use, we recommend you read the blue inserts found throughout the book. The hard data in Part 4 will also help you make the case for implementing CAL.

How to read this book?

Throughout the book, you'll find inserts with testimonials or practical examples of CAL.

Part 2 features a real-life example of a CAL group and the topic it addresses that's used to illustrate each step of the method, one short chapter at a time.

Part 2 also includes a description of each step, its objectives, and benefits and outlines how the steps can be facilitated. Facilitation tips, for challenging situations, are also provided. A summary table describes the role of each participant – client, consultant, facilitator – and what they need to do.

For readers who want to know more about the research behind the method and how it has evolved, to complement the practical information and real-life story, the authors also provide some background and suggestions for further reading; to find these, look for the book symbols.

The learning journals found throughout the book are intended to help you with your reflective practice, so you ask the right questions from the get-go.

Reference

1. World Economic Forum. (2023). *The future of jobs report 2023*. World Economic Forum. https://www.weforum.org/reports/the-future-of-jobs-report-2023/

Part 1

**Codevelopment
Action Learning**

Overview of the approach

1

What is the Codevelopment Action Learning approach?

In an increasingly fast-paced world, Codevelopment Action Learning (CAL) invites people to take the time to share openly, focus and reflect, and learn from each other.

Concretely, CAL organizes people into groups. Five to eight people come together with a common purpose: namely, to **co-create** solutions, **accelerate** their goals, and **grow** through mutual learning. Over the course of several weeks, months, or even years, participants meet on a regular basis to explore real-life and work situations, such as projects, goals, decisions, and challenges. The group works as a team to explore new possibilities and initiate change. More importantly, everyone builds their capacities by learning from each of the real-life situations brought by and to the group.

CAL acts as a springboard for people, groups, teams, and organizations, in the sense that the group leverages the strengths and expertise of each participant to create innovative solutions and give them the confidence to move forward.

Since CAL groups usually meet several times, participants have the opportunity to reflect on the actions they took between sessions, assess the outcomes, learn from them, and find new ways to grow.

It takes time to develop problem-solving, leadership skills, and the ability to reflect. Reading, for instance, won't help you much if you want to improve your communication skills, which are key to **co-creating**, collaborating, and building the relationships that help you innovate and grow in a complex world. The same goes for soft skills like curiosity, open-mindedness, and leadership that open up possibilities and help you **accelerate** your goals, or resilience that helps you **grow**, even when confronted with rapid change. This is where CAL's hands-on approach comes in.

DOI: 10.4324/9781032625720-3

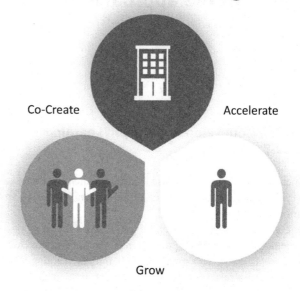

Figure 1.1 Codevelopment Action Learning objectives.

CAL's objectives: co-create, accelerate, and grow

Practically speaking, how can CAL help both individuals and groups, as well as teams and organizations, meet their goals? Simply by focusing on three main objectives: co-create, accelerate, and grow (see Figure 1.1).

To illustrate these objectives, let's imagine a scenario where a large engineering company has won a contract to build a high-speed suspended monorail in a nearby city. The company must restructure in order to promote cross-functional collaboration between its internal departments and external partners. Moreover, it hasn't been immune to the effects of labour shortage, as it looks to hire from a shrinking labour pool after many of its senior staff retired. In response to this challenge, the directors decided to set up CAL groups for all their managers.

We'll return to this example many times in Part 2, as it's used to illustrate each of the steps in the method. But, before discussing it in this part, let's first look at what led the directors to choose CAL.

Co-create: creativity and collaboration

The directors chose CAL because it encourages participants to share and be open to other points of view and a variety of experiences.

The resulting collective intelligence gives participants new ways of looking at situations.

For example, the managers taking part in CAL co-create solutions that help resolve the challenges they face in their day-to-day lives, or with their work teams, much more effectively than if they were trying to deal with them on their own.[1–4]

Moreover, by including managers from different sectors in the CAL groups, the directors are helping break down organizational silos.[5–7] In fact, CAL forges new cross-functional collaboration channels, [8,9] a key factor in speeding up the company's highly complex, cross-disciplinary project.

The restructuring and need to hire new managers are also significant challenges. When new challenges arise every day, and become progressively harder to solve, people often tend to feel isolated. In CAL, the directors saw a way of giving their managers a safe space where they could co-create and innovate, but that would also act as an incubator for a culture of social support – a vital asset for reducing work-related stress.[8,10]

Now, let's take a look at how co-creation is the foundation on which CAL's two main outcomes rest: reaching goals faster and growing.

Accelerate: reach goals faster, complete projects more efficiently

The directors' primary goal is to realign the company for optimal performance and build the monorail on time and on budget. The support provided by the CAL groups give their leaders the collective intelligence and creativity they need to be more confident and pro-active. The experiences shared in the groups also enable them to make better decisions faster, based on learning about their co-workers' different experiences, as well as taking the time to think and reflect – something that, caught up in their busy lives, they generally don't stop to do.

Most leaders who take part in CAL sessions develop a greater understanding of their own role in the company, as well as the role of their co-workers, which strengthens their professional identity.[11] However, the most significant benefit is that, by combining their strengths and being open to new ways of thinking, people and teams can accelerate their goals and bring their projects to a successful conclusion.

The outcome our directors are hoping for is that their managers will have an increased sense of self-efficacy, enabling them to become more pro-active.[10,12]

Grow: elevate and capability building

Of course, successfully implementing the monorail project will involve harnessing a wide range of technical and technological knowledge and skills. But, completing it efficiently and effectively will require the often overlooked human capabilities. The directors chose CAL because, in addition to developing cognitive skills, such as analytical and divergent thinking, creativity, problem-solving, reflection, and communication skills, such as listening, questioning, and giving feedback, it's also known for helping to develop capabilities such as leadership and resilience.[11,12]

Promoting personal growth among members is a key component of organizational transformation, that will contribute to effective teamwork and cross-sector collaboration. After all, restructuring and other large-scale projects take time, and our changing environments mean that employees will inevitably have to adapt to other major changes, at which point the skills learned in CAL will prove their worth.

Because participants leave CAL sessions, return to their daily routine, and then go back to CAL, the approach enables them to put what they learn into practice. Participants also integrate those lessons with what they learn from more traditional professional development methods, such as conferences, leadership forums, coaching, and self-directed e-learning.

Implementing CAL over a period of time and throughout the organization helps establish and maintain a learning culture.[5,7] As the directors in our scenario know, the method's spin-off benefits include: improved performance, maintaining the organization's competitive advantage in the face of constant change, and the positive impact on society as a whole of training the workforce.[13-15]

The origins and evolution of Codevelopment Action Learning

Research shows that traditional, classroom-based lectures are not the best teaching method for most adult learners.[16] Rather, adults learn best when they're able to experience, problem-solve, and reflect on their actions, and when learning is directly related to their work and/ or personal life.

Taking this into account, Adrien Payette, Management Professor, and Claude Champagne, OD professional/manager, published their first book in 1997 on Professional Codevelopment groups (their initial name, abbreviated to CDGs), now Codevelopment Action Learning (CAL).

The inspiration for CDGs came from a variety of existing theories and practices: Action Learning,[17,18] Experiential Learning,[19,20] Reflective Practice and Action Science,[21,22] consulting,[23,24] and the Learning Organization.[25]

In the past two decades, CDGs have taken off in the French-speaking world, gradually establishing themselves in many public and private sector organizations in Canada, France, and Belgium.[5,7,12]

In the 2000s, the authors focussed primarily on writing articles that introduced the method, explained how to implement it, showed its versatility, and presented various success stories.[26-28]

Between 2010 and 2020, as the CDG method became more popular, other authors such as Nathalie Sabourin and France Lefebvre, and university researchers such as Nathalie Lafranchise and Maxime Paquet, began looking at new ways to successfully implement the method and measure its outcomes at both the individual and organizational level.[7,8,11]

Inspired by social constructivism, appreciative inquiry, positive psychology, and French works on peer-based support[29–32] (such as counselling, coaching, apprenticeship, mentoring, and tutoring), we focussed our work on finding ways to help facilitators develop their peer-based support skills and empowering leadership so that they, in turn, can support the CAL group, as well as guiding the sessions.[11,33–35] In fact, facilitating the seven steps is a relatively easy task for an experienced facilitator, but managing to promote participants' learning and development during and between sessions is another matter!

We recently wrote a scientific article on a large-scale, online CAL event that was attended by participants from throughout the French-speaking world.[36] Writing it enabled us to define the similarities and differences between CAL and traditional action learning. In academic circles, the current definition of CAL is as follows:

> CAL groups are small groups where participants learn from each other and co-create solutions they will apply at work. Group members use real life situations – projects, dreams, goals, decisions, or challenges to be overcome – as a way of developing their professional and personal capabilities. The most important aspect of CAL groups is that participants focus on collaborating, learning, reflecting and transferring what they have learned into action. In other words, participants work while learning and learn while working. CAL groups can also generate positive change in teams, groups and organizations.[36] (p. 2)

Learning journal

What does your current context require?

If you were in a CAL group, what topics would you like to discuss?

What are the benefits of the CAL approach for you, your team leaders, and the other members of your organization?

References

1. Arnaud, B., & Caruso Cahn, S. (2016). *La boîte à outils de l'intelligence collective*. Dunod.
2. Austissier, D., Johnson, D. J., & Moutot, J.-M. (2018). *L'innovation managériale*. Eyrolles.
3. Slade, S. (2018). *Going horizontal: Creating non-hierarchical organizations, one practice at a time* (1st ed.). Berrett-Koehler Publishers, Inc.
4. Lipmanowicz, H., & McCandless, K. (2013). *The surprising power of liberating structures: Simple rules to unleash a culture of innovation*. Liberating Structures Press.
5. Hoffner-Lesure, A., & Delaunay, D. (2011). *Le codéveloppement professionnel et managérial l'approche qui rend acteur et développe l'intelligence collective*. Éditions EMS, Management & société.
6. Payette, A. (2011). Codéveloppement et changement organisationnel. In A. Hoffner-Lesure & D. Delaunay (Eds.), *Le codéveloppement professionnel et managérial l'approche qui rend acteur et développe l'intelligence collective* (pp. 211–247). Éditions EMS, Management & société.
7. Sabourin, N., & Lefebvre, F. (2017). *Collaborer et agir: Mieux et autrement: Guide pratique pour implanter des groupes de codéveloppement professionnel*. Éditions Sabourin Lefebvre.
8. Paquet, M., & Lafranchise, N. (2014). La recherche sur les groupes de codéveloppement professionnel: Un objet en émergence. *Magazine Effectif, 17*(1), 26–27.
9. Paquet, M., & Lafranchise, N. (2020). Le groupe de codéveloppement professionnel: Vecteur d'apprentissage et d'efficacité personnelle par la prise en compte des émotions. In M. Saint-Jean & M. Paquet (Eds.), *Émotions et compétences émotionnelles dans l'activité professionnelle et la formation* (pp. 131–162). L'Harmattan.
10. Paquet, M., Lafranchise, N., & Sabourin, N. (2021). Des contributions d'une recherche-action pour le codéveloppement. In C. Champagne (Ed.), *Le groupe de codéveloppement. La puissance de l'intelligence collective* (pp. 228–234). Presses de l'Université du Québec.
11. Lafranchise, N., & Paquet, M. (2020). Accompagner des animateurs de groupes de codéveloppement professionnel, dans des milieux de la santé au Québec, dans une visée d'optimisation du rôle. In M. Saint-Jean & V. LeBlanc (Eds.), *Formation des professionnels de santé, partenariat patient. Vers une perspective humaniste* (pp. 123–147). L'Harmattan.
12. Champagne, C. (2021). *Le groupe de codéveloppement: La puissance de l'intelligence collective*. Presses de l'Université du Québec.
13. Kim, K., & Lu, Z. (2019). Learning organization and organizational performance. In A. R. Örtenblad (Ed.), *The Oxford handbook of the learning organization* (pp. 332–346). Oxford University Press.

14. Marsick, V. J., & Watkins, K. E. (2003). Demonstrating the value of an organization's learning culture: The dimensions of the learning organization questionnaire. *Advances in Developing Human Resources, 5*(2), 132–151. https://doi.org/10.1177/1523422303005002002
15. Watkins, K. E., & Marsick, V. J. (2019). Conceptualizing an organization that learns. In A. R. Örtenblad (Ed.), *The Oxford handbook of the learning organization* (pp. 50–66). Oxford University Press.
16. Knowles, M. S., Holton, E. F., & Swanson, R. A. (2015). *The adult learner: The definitive classic in adult education and human resource development* (8th ed.). Routledge.
17. McGill, I., & Beaty, L. (2001). *Action learning: A guide for professional, management & educational development* (2nd ed., rev.). Kogan Page; Stylus Pub.
18. Revans, R. W. (1982). *The origins and growths of action learning*. Krieger Publishing Company.
19. Kolb, D. A. (2015). *Experiential learning: Experience as the source of learning and development* (2nd ed.). Pearson Education, Inc.
20. Peterson, K., & Kolb, D. A. (2017). *How you learn is how you live: Using nine ways of learning to transform your life*. Berrett-Koehler Publishers, Inc.
21. Argyris, C., Putnam, R., & Smith, D. M. (1985). *Action science* (1st ed.). Jossey-Bass.
22. Schön, D. A. (2017). *The reflective practitioner: How professionals think in action*. Routledge.
23. Lescarbeau, R., Payette, M., & Saint-Arnaud, Y. (2004). *Profession consultant*. Gaëtan Morin.
24. Schein, E. H. (1995). Process consultation, action research and clinical inquiry: Are they the same? *Journal of Managerial Psychology, 10*(6), 14–19. https://doi.org/10.1108/02683949510093830
25. Senge, P. M. (2006). *The fifth discipline: The art and practice of the learning organization* (Rev. and updated). Doubleday/Currency.
26. Champagne, C. (2001). Trois pistes pour enrichir la pratique du groupe de codéveloppement. *Interactions, 5*(2), 99–110.
27. Payette, A. (2000). Le codéveloppement: Une approche graduée. *Interactions, 4*(2), 39–59.
28. Tétreault, B. (2001). Une formidable expérience de formation. *Interactions, 5*(2), 53–54.
29. Paul, M. (2016). *La démarche d'accompagnement. Repères méthodologiques et ressources théoriques*. De Boeck Supérieur.
30. Lafortune, L., Lepage, C., & Persechino, F. (2008). *Compétences professionnelles pour l'accompagnement d'un changement: Un référentiel*. Presses de l'Université du Québec.
31. Cooperrider, D. L., Zandee, D. P., Godwin, L. N., Avital, M., & Boland, B. (Eds.). (2013). *Organizational generativity: The appreciative inquiry summit and a scholarship of transformation* (1st ed.). Emerald.

32. Quinn, R. E. (2015). *The positive organization: Breaking free from conventional cultures, constraints, and beliefs* (1st ed.). Berrett-Koehler Publishers, Inc.

33. Cheong, M., Yammarino, F. J., Dionne, S. D., Spain, S. M., & Tsai, C.-Y. (2019). A review of the effectiveness of empowering leadership. *The Leadership Quarterly, 30*(1), 34–58. https://doi.org/10.1016/j.leaqua.2018.08.005

34. Lafranchise, N., Paquet, M., Gagné, M.-J., & Cadec, K. (2019). Accompagner les animateurs pour optimiser les groupes de codéveloppement. In F. Vandercleyen, M.-J. Dumoulin, & J. Desjardins (Eds.), *Former à l'accompagnement de stagiaires par le codéveloppement professionnel: Conditions, défis et perspectives* (pp. 155–182). Presses de l'Université du Québec.

35. Paquet, M., Lafranchise, N., Gagné, M.-J., & Cadec, K. (2017). La rétroaction. Une manière de développer une posture de leadership d'accompagnement chez des personnes animatrices de groupes de codéveloppement. In M. Saint-Jean, N. Lafranchise, C. Lepage, & L. Lafortune (Eds.), *Regards croisés sur la rétroaction et le débriefing: Accompagner, former et professionnaliser* (pp. 57–76). Presses de l'Université du Québec.

36. Paquet, M., Sabourin, N., Lafranchise, N., Cheshire, R., & Pelbois, J. (2022). Codevelopment Action Learning during the pandemic – findings from two online co-learning and co-creation events: Twenty Codevelopment Action Learning sessions were held simultaneously for 148 participants from nine French-speaking countries. *Action Learning: Research and Practice, 19*(1), 19–32. https://doi.org/10.1080/14767333.2022.2026761

How it works

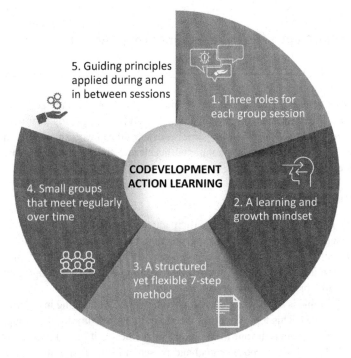

2

The five key components

By now, you must be wondering: "So, how does Codevelopment Action Learning (CAL) actually work?"

Concretely, the approach is based on five key components (see Figure 2.1):

Component 1: Three roles for each group session
Component 2: A learning and growth mindset
Component 3: A structured yet flexible 7-step method
Component 4: Small groups meet regularly over time
Component 5: Guiding principles applied during and in between sessions

Figure 2.1 The five key components of CAL.

DOI: 10.4324/9781032625720-4

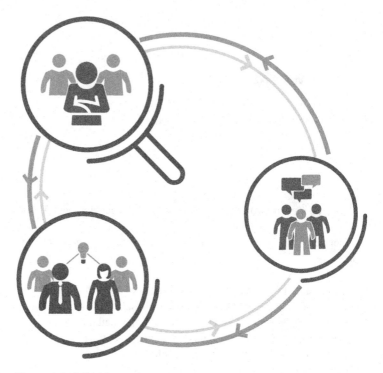

Figure 2.2 CAL's three roles.

Component 1: three roles for each group session

A key feature of a CAL group is the three roles: client, consultants, and facilitator (see Figure 2.2).[1–3]

Because each participant has a specific role, CAL groups are a lot more effective than a discussion group, a meeting, or a get-together over coffee. In fact, everyone who participates must do so with an open mind and the will to **co-create** solutions, **accelerate** their goals, and **grow** through mutual learning.

The client

For each CAL session, one participant takes on the client role; this person is supported by the other group members (Figure 2.3).

The client presents a work-related topic to the group. Possible topics include achieving a goal, fast-tracking a project, making an important decision, or overcoming a challenge.

The topic is a real situation that needs new ways of thinking in order to be resolved. This topic becomes the learning opportunity for the group. While the client is the one to choose the topic, ideally, it should be aligned with the group's purpose or goal and present a learning opportunity for all participants (see Part 2 for more information about the topic.)

Figure 2.3 The client role in a CAL group.

Except for the facilitator, at the start of each session, participants take turns assuming the client role. The client is usually chosen before the session, i.e., at launch, at the end of the previous session or at the start of the subsequent one.

Because the client is a crucial part of the process, they must do some advance thinking and preparation (see Chapter 4/Step 0 in Part 2). Being able to count on a group that will spend time listening and helping is a privilege. In return, clients must choose a topic that's consistent with the group's purpose and will provide learning opportunities for the other participants. So, before the session starts, assisted by the facilitator, the client can kickstart the learning process by asking themselves questions, reflecting on the topic, choosing it, and refining it.

The consultants

Once the client has been chosen by the group, the other participants take on the role of consultants (see Figure 2.4).

Figure 2.4 The consultant role in a CAL group.

Consultants wear two hats during a CAL session:

–   **Catalyst**: The consultants' genuine interest in the client's topic inspires the client to think and act. By asking clarifying, open-ended questions, they spark new ideas. They can also share their experiences and points of view, express new ideas, and offer solutions and/or practical support in a respectful manner.
–   **Learner**: Just like the client, the consultants come to the CAL group to grow and learn. They either learn from the topic brought

by the client or about the CAL approach itself. Or they might develop other capabilities that are central to CAL, such as active listening, effective questioning, reflective practice, divergent thinking, and so on. These skills are further discussed in Part 2.

While consultants help resolve the issue presented by the client, this is not their only job. Consultants also have a more reflective role, in that they look at the issue in context, as well as different aspects of the client's situation. The topic is also a learning opportunity for them.[2]

In the CAL method, the group doesn't try and reach a consensus or impose a unique solution. Rather, consultants listen, then ask relevant questions to help the client clarify their situation. Then, they provide the client with support by sharing ideas and solutions, based on their own experience. They can also offer different kinds of practical support to help the client move forward.

Through these discussions and the resulting insights, both the client and consultants learn and integrate relevant ideas they can apply to their own situation.

Because consultants usually come from different backgrounds, they bring different kinds of expertise to the group. Whatever their professional background or skills, they actively listen, try to understand, ask questions, support and reflect, rather than acting like an expert who simply wants to display their knowledge.

One of a consultant's core skills is active listening, demonstrated by such behaviours as keeping silent, reflecting, and reframing. Consultants also ask thoughtful and supportive questions and provide constructive feedback.

The type of questions asked during a CAL session and the kind of the information shared directly impact the sessions' success and also how supported the client feels.

CAL consultants don't need any formal training to take on that role. Rather, they learn as they go along, supported by the facilitator, as needed. See Part 2 for more information about the consultant's role at each of the different steps.

The facilitator

> "Facilitators make learning easy."
>
> Ron Cheshire[3]

The third role in a CAL group is that of the facilitator (Figure 2.5). CAL facilitators take on the role of a guide who encourages learning and co-creation.

The facilitator uses the CAL method to guide the group discussion and promotes a healthy group dynamic.

Most importantly, the facilitator ensures that the learning process is ongoing over time,[3] and that the group is much more than a problem-solving meeting.

Figure 2.5 The facilitator role in a CAL group.

The role of the facilitator is to help participants achieve their own goals, as well as the ones set by the group and the organization, one example of which might be focusing on specific leadership skills. They use interactive facilitation techniques to spark creative thinking, generate insights, ensure participants are aware of what they've learned – and how they can apply those insights at work.

The facilitator encourages the other participants to take on some responsibilities, such as organizing ice-breaker activities or reserving the meeting room. They also ensure that a process is in place to assess and record the group's results and outcomes.

Facilitators usually help clients go through the preparation in Step 0 (see component 3) and also keep track of topics covered, participant goals, courses of action, and lessons learned. They can also provide feedback and share resources that can help the group achieve its learning goals. Unlike the client and consultant roles, which the participants take turns assuming, generally speaking, the facilitator's role doesn't change.

In short, the role of the facilitator is very important to CAL as they ensure that the group follows the guiding principles and method, explained below.

See Part 2 for more information about the role and responsibilities of the facilitator. Also, Chapter 15 in Part 3 provides more details about how to choose, recruit, and train CAL facilitators.

Facilitation tips – organizational culture and adaptations

It is important to note that the names "client" and "consultant" used in CAL are neutral and do not imply any commercial implications.

However, in some organizational cultures, these names may not be appropriate, due to their common usage or perceived meaning. For example, in a community-based social sector organization, practitioners have replaced "client" with "guided person" and "consultant" with "guide." Based on our experience, we also use the terms "client-coachee" and "consultant-coach" for better acceptance, when needed.[8]

Component 2: a learning and growth mindset

Participating in a CAL group requires setting aside one's preconceptions and adopting a growth mindset.[4] With the other participants' help, group members must be willing to set learning intentions and to embark on a process of continuous learning and growth regarding their leadership, capabilities, and their overall performance (see Figure 2.6).

Participants must also develop an inquiry attitude,[5] which involves stepping back and being humble when participating in group discussions. Challenging their own beliefs and actions is a necessary part of expanding their horizons. Every participant must have this mindset, as they will take turns assuming the client role.

Developing an inquiry attitude is also a way for participants to show that they value their co-workers' experience. After all, there are innumerable easily available resources designed to boost leadership and capabilities, but actually putting that knowledge into practice can be a challenge. Real work experience is a powerful tool for transferring skills that are difficult to learn simply by reading books.

To foster these qualities in participants, the CAL group must be a safe space with a learning mindset, where a positive group dynamic prevails. We therefore suggest that you avoid recruiting people who are

Figure 2.6 CAL's learning and growth mindset.

experiencing workplace conflict or other sensitive issues. CAL is not a conflict resolution group. Although CAL groups can and do support team building and cooperation, their value lies in the learning and increasing the effectiveness of its members.

Finally, participating in a CAL group means putting the theoretical learning into practice between sessions in order to make more progress. In fact, it's that commitment to action that makes all the difference; to achieve it, they need a growth mindset that will stay with them when they leave the sessions and accompany them throughout their day. Practically speaking, this means they will become more effective, complete their projects and reach their goals faster, and find new ways to resolve everyday challenges at work.

Component 3: a structured yet flexible seven-step method

The CAL method has the benefit of being both structured and flexible. As shown below, there are seven steps, plus a preparation phrase called Step 0. To achieve the maximum benefits with regard to learning, creativity, and action, these steps must be followed in the exact order, from 0 to 7 (see Figure 2.7).

While these deceptively simple steps are easy to follow, when put into practice, they yield surprisingly strong results, and these results are enhanced by the group's synergy.

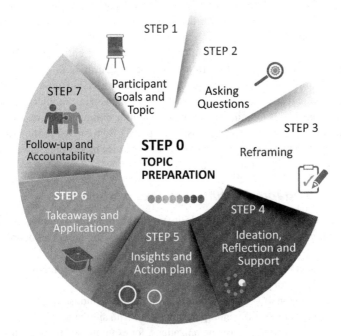

Figure 2.7 CAL's seven-step method.

The structure and time limit of each step makes for a more effective group discussion. Indeed, participants are often surprised that they managed to resolve a complicated issue in such a short period of time, as well as learning from that issue and gaining insights they can apply to their own work.

Excluding the time spent on Step 0, CAL sessions usually last around 90 minutes. Ideally, sessions should be incorporated into a two- to three-hour workshop, held either in person or online. That way, there will be time left over for related activities such as learning modules, sharing resources, check-in activities, and midway review.[6]

In order to get the most out of CAL, the session should focus on a single client. Sessions with several clients tend to devolve into problem-solving; real learning requires more focused and mindful attention, which also promotes individual and collective development.

See Part 2 for more information on each of the seven steps.

Component 4: small groups that meet regularly over time

Small groups

Our research and experience has shown that the ideal number of participants for in-person groups is six or seven, plus a facilitator,[1,7] while five or six participants (plus a facilitator) is the right number for online groups.[8]

CAL is a good choice for groups of leaders and managers, experts, professionals, and teams. See the Table, below, for a list of potential participants.

As shown in Table 2.1, group composition can be either uniform or diverse, depending on the group's (or the organization's) objectives. For example, one group could be part of a leadership development program and consist exclusively of first-line managers. Another group, where the goal is to build the company's multidisciplinary culture, could rally nurses, doctors, psychologists, and people from related professions around a common objective: changing their service model in response to an institutional reorganization.

Can be adapted to different circumstances

One of CAL's key features is its ability to adapt to different circumstances, meaning you can use the approach with the following groups of people:

- Leaders or project managers from the same organization but different departments or teams
- Professionals (IT, for example), from the same industry/sector
- Leaders from different organizations but with similar professions (HR leaders from large organizations, for example, or entrepreneurs)

Leaders and managers	Experts and professionals	Teams
To develop leadership and management skills	*To share expertise, promote creativity and collaboration*	*To solve the team's mission-related situations*
Entrepreneurs	Professionals such as HR employees, accountants, engineers, nurses, doctors, psychologists, educational counsellors, etc.	Management teams
Executives		Project teams
Management		Natural teams
Middle management		Leadership forums with executives or managers
Coordinators		
Team leaders	Mentors	
Project managers	Academics	
Supervisors	Consultants	
High-potential team members	Coaches and facilitators	

Table 2.1 Potential CAL participants

– People in the educational sector: teachers who want to learn from each other, graduate students, or even undergraduates, during a class

Implementing CAL in a management forum

CAL can also be implemented in large groups, which are divided into smaller, simultaneous groups. Several sessions have been held simultaneously at large management forums,[8] at training seminars, and during the launch phase of a community of practice for HR professionals.

Meets regularly over time

Participating in a CAL group means being part of a learning journey that spans several sessions. Participants meet at regular, consecutive intervals – anywhere from two to six weeks – over time. The number of meetings is chosen by the group depending on its needs. Participants can use the time between sessions to put what they've learned into practice.

Ideally, there should be at least as many sessions as there are participants, so everyone has a chance to take on the client role. We also recommend adding a kickoff session at the beginning and a wrap-up meeting at the end, to assess the results, decide if the group will continue, and look for potential future facilitators. This pre-set number of meetings is equivalent to one CAL "cycle" (see Figure 2.8).

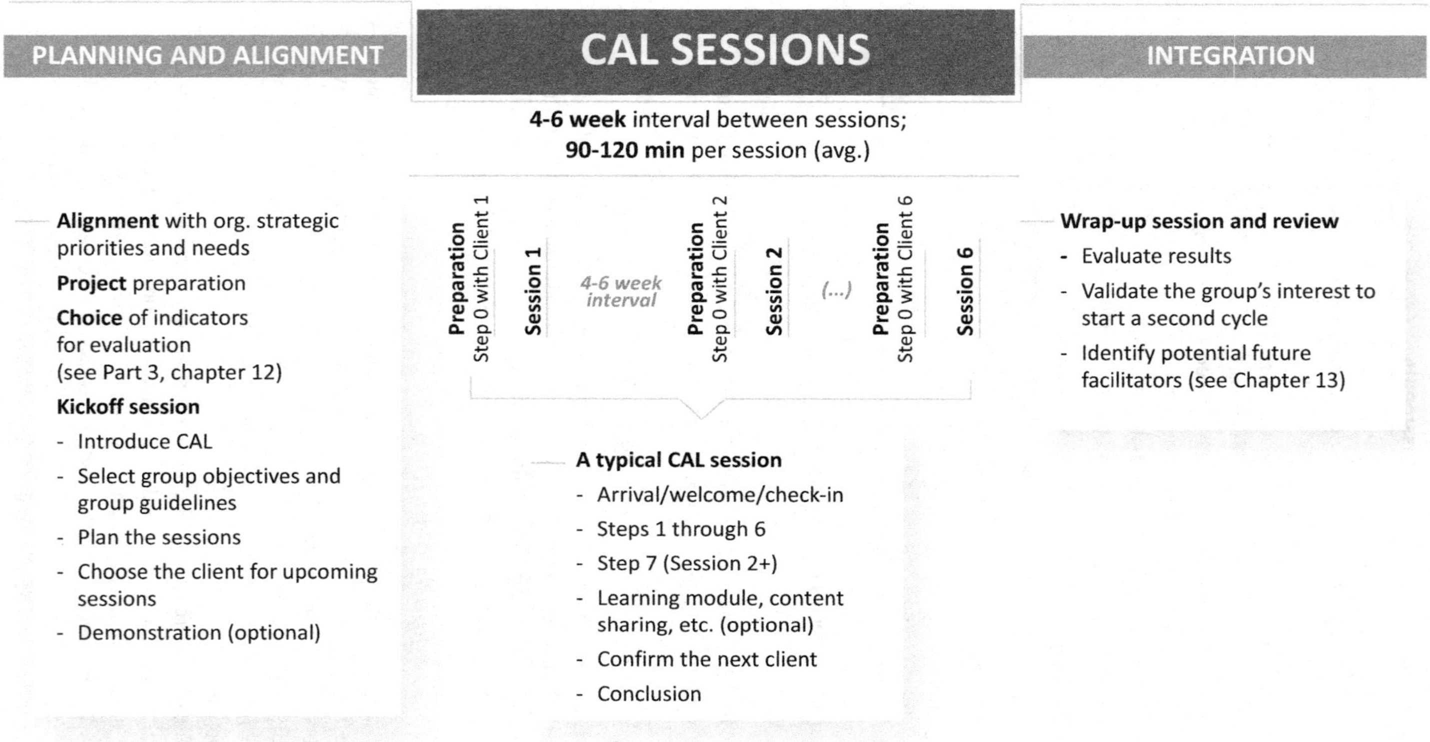

PLANNING AND ALIGNMENT

Alignment with org. strategic priorities and needs

Project preparation

Choice of indicators for evaluation (see Part 3, chapter 12)

Kickoff session

- Introduce CAL
- Select group objectives and group guidelines
- Plan the sessions
- Choose the client for upcoming sessions
- Demonstration (optional)

CAL SESSIONS

4-6 week interval between sessions; **90-120 min** per session (avg.)

Preparation
Step 0 with Client 1

Session 1

4-6 week interval

Preparation
Step 0 with Client 2

Session 2

(...)

Preparation
Step 0 with Client 6

Session 6

A typical CAL session

- Arrival/welcome/check-in
- Steps 1 through 6
- Step 7 (Session 2+)
- Learning module, content sharing, etc. (optional)
- Confirm the next client
- Conclusion

INTEGRATION

Wrap-up session and review

- Evaluate results
- Validate the group's interest to start a second cycle
- Identify potential future facilitators (see Chapter 13)

Figure 2.2 A CAL learning journey

Facilitation tips – number and duration of CAL sessions

In a situation where resources are limited, for example, or a pilot project is being implemented, we have observed that the CAL approach can deliver positive results with as few as five or six consecutive, spaced-out sessions.

A CAL session usually lasts between 90 and 120 minutes. More time can be added for connexion, sharing of resources and of course, breaks. Many facilitators organize half-day CAL workshops.

So, a group of six managers wanting to build their leadership skills could plan to meet eight times over the course of a year or every six weeks. Another group, this one consisting of seven project leaders in charge of an urgent reorganization project could decide to meet every three weeks. After meeting seven times over a six-month period, the group could declare the first cycle finished, assess their progress, and check people's interest in starting a second cycle.

Our experience has shown that the greater the number of sessions, the more in-depth the learning insights. If they feel the need and have the resources, groups can stay together for more than one cycle. As mentioned, CAL has the potential to deliver significant positive impacts. However, there's a direct connection between those impacts and the time participants spend together.

Figure 2.8 illustrates a typical CAL cycle for six participants and their facilitator. The cycle consists of six sessions, plus a kickoff session and a wrap-up meeting.

Component 5: guiding principles applied during and in between sessions

Just as a key component of high-performing teams is their level of trust, effective CAL groups are characterized by an environment that's conducive to learning.

CAL's three main guiding principles (see Figure 2.9) are that all participants must[3]:

1. **Be committed to the group**. This is voluntary and stems from each participant's personal sense of responsibility.
2. **Be collaborative and supportive**. This is based on an attitude of mutual goodwill, openness, and trust.
3. **Be respectful and discrete**. This applies to all personal, confidential details discussed in the group.

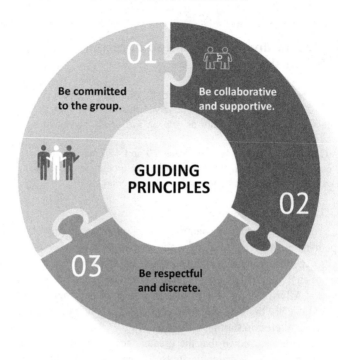

Figure 2.9 CAL's three guiding principles.

The CAL group must become a safe space that encourages openness, creativity, ongoing development, and the right to make mistakes and learn from them.[6,9]

The whole group must abide by these principles, as they are key to CAL's success. It's partly because of them that the groups are a place where participants can feel free to express themselves openly and talk about their challenges and goals. In order to do so, participants cannot be held back by fear of judgement or criticism. But creating an atmosphere of trust isn't just the facilitator's job. Everyone is responsible for ensuring the group adheres to these values, not just during the sessions, but between them and even after the cycle (or cycles) are over.

In this chapter, we've looked at the five key components the approach is based on: the three roles, the mindset, the seven-step method and the guiding principles, and examined in greater detail the fact that the approach is implemented in small groups, that can be adapted to different circumstances, and that meet regularly over time of time.

Learning journal

In your organization, who do you think would get the most out of CAL?

How can you create a climate of learning in your groups?

Which managers, leaders, or other participants could you recruit to test the approach?

References

1. Champagne, C. (2021). *Le groupe de codéveloppement: La puissance de l'intelligence collective*. Presses de l'Université du Québec.
2. Payette, A., & Champagne, C. (1997). *Le groupe de codéveloppement professionnel*. Presses de l'Université du Québec.
3. Sabourin, N., & Lefebvre, F. (2017). *Collaborer et agir: Mieux et autrement: Guide pratique pour implanter des groupes de codéveloppement professionnel*. Éditions Sabourin Lefebvre.
4. Dweck, C. (2016). *What having a "Growth Mindset" actually means*. Harvard Business Review. https://hbr.org/2016/01/what-having-a-growth-mindset-actually-means
5. Adams, M. G. (2022). *Change your questions, change your life: 10 powerful tools for life and work* (4th ed.). Berrett-Koehler Publishers.
6. Paquet, M., & Lafranchise, N. (2020). Le groupe de codéveloppement professionnel: Vecteur d'apprentissage et d'efficacité personnelle par la prise en compte des émotions. In M. Saint-Jean & M. Paquet (Eds.), Émotions et compétences émotionnelles dans l'activité professionnelle et la formation (pp. 131–162). L'Harmattan.
7. Paquet, M., Lafranchise, N., Gagné, M.-J., & Cadec, K. (2017). La rétroaction. Une manière de développer une posture de leadership d'accompagnement chez des personnes animatrices de groupes de codéveloppement. In M. Saint-Jean, N. Lafranchise, C. Lepage, & L. Lafortune (Eds.), Regards croisés sur la rétroaction et le débriefing : *Accompagner, former et professionnaliser* (pp. 57–76). Presses de l'Université du Québec.

8. Paquet, M., Sabourin, N., Lafranchise, N., Cheshire, R., & Pelbois, J. (2022). Codevelopment Action Learning during the pandemic – findings from two online co-learning and co-creation events: Twenty Codevelopment Action Learning sessions were held simultaneously for 148 participants from nine French-speaking countries. *Action Learning: Research and Practice*, *19*(1), 19–32. https://doi.org/10.1080/14767333.2022.2026761

9. Lafranchise, N., & Paquet, M. (2020). Accompagner des animateurs de groupes de codéveloppement professionnel, dans des milieux de la santé au Québec, dans une visée d'optimisation du rôle. In M. Saint-Jean & V. LeBlanc (Eds.), *Formation des professionnels de santé, partenariat patient. Vers une perspective humaniste* (pp. 123–147). L'Harmattan.

The Codevelopment Action Learning Method

Part 2

Introduction to the steps

3

As shown in Figure 3.1, the Codevelopment Action Learning (CAL) method includes seven steps that give shape to the group session. Also, the client prepares a topic during Step 0, prior to the CAL session.

Each chapter has an "Example," part of a real-life story showing how CAL evolves. Following Emilio's case as he and his group proceed through the steps provides a practical illustration of the method. The story starts here.

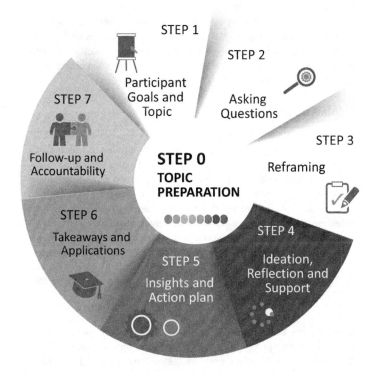

Figure 3.1 CAL's seven-step method.

DOI: 10.4324/9781032625720-6

A forthcoming CAL session

Emilio is the Director of Operations at a large engineering company. The company needs to restructure to take advantage of the new transportation options being built in the city. Also, to speed up new product development, it must break down silos and promote cross-functional collaboration.

The company is also going through a wave of retirements among its managers. New leaders will need to be onboarded quickly and become aligned with the company's vision.

A new challenge

For Emilio, strategic planning, networking, and change management are the favourite parts of his job. He's an experienced manager, easy-going, and trustworthy, who prefers action over stability. He's known for having built a successful team and for his direct leadership style. While Emilio is generally patient and tolerant, he gets annoyed when members of his team are reluctant to get engaged or leave their comfort zones. In his opinion, this is a major obstacle to progress, especially in the ever-changing world of engineering. One of his favourite sayings is: "Adapt and prosper or get left behind."

Following the company's strategic leadership off-site, Emilio is assigned to a new project – building a citywide, high-speed suspended monorail – that will require him to collaborate cross-functionally with every other department. He will also need to lead his team of first-level managers, which includes many new, young faces.

Joining a CAL group

To support leaders through the restructuring process, the CEO and senior management had the idea of forming a pilot CAL group for the directors. Why CAL? It would give managers with new strategic projects a place where they could strengthen their leadership capabilities and find solutions to concrete challenges. CAL would also speed up the implementation of cross-functional initiatives and create a supportive community for leaders to share meaningful experiences. It would also act as a think tank to generate ideas for further projects, and a pilot to see if CAL could be deployed in other teams or levels of management.

The VP of HR suggested the pilot CAL group be named the Transformation and Leadership Group.

****

A few weeks before the first CAL session, a kickoff meeting was held with the six prospective participants and their facilitator, Barb. During the session, the six directors stated their goals and how they wanted to proceed. Barb explained the CAL approach and method, and the group chose the person who would take on the client role in the upcoming sessions.

Emilio volunteered to be the first one to take on that role. "*If we want this thing to work, we have to lead by example!*" he said enthusiastically.*

***

The group's facilitator, Barb, is a seasoned and dynamic external consultant who has been trained as a CAL facilitator and has experience working with senior leaders. Several senior managers knew of her experience, so she was asked to facilitate the pilot group.

How to read Chapters 4–11

Chapters 4–11 give a comprehensive description of the CAL method's seven steps, including Step 0, the preparation phase (see Table 3.1).

Chapter/step	Objectives	Suggested time (total: ≈90–120 min)
Chapter 4: Step 0 – Topic Preparation (*Takes place before the session*)	Organize ideas, summarize the topic's most important points, and express a precise need to the group. Identify the topic's relevance for the group.	Brief discussion, max. 30 min.
Chapter 5: Step 1 – Participant Goals and Topic	Briefly present the goals/ learning intentions (all participants). Summarize the topic (client).	≈20 min.
Chapter 6: Step 2 – Asking Questions	Clarify the topic for the group and stimulate the client's reflection process.	≈20 min.
Chapter 7: Step 3 – Reframing	Stimulates reflection on the topic and openness to new perspectives. Reframing must include the client's goal and their request for support from the group.	≈15 min.
Chapter 8: Step 4 – Ideation, Reflection, and Support	Help the client find new ways of seeing and thinking about their topic and offer support.	≈20 min.

(Continued)

Chapter/step	Objectives	Suggested time (total: ≈90–120 min)
Chapter 9: Step 5 – Insights and Action Plan	Identify concrete, short- and medium-term, achievable actions.	≈10 min.
Chapter 10: Step 6 – Takeaways and Actions	Discuss the group's Acquisitions, share their Actions, and give their Assessment.	≈20 min.
Chapter 11: Step 7 – Follow-up and Accountability (Session 2+)	Follow up on how the client implemented their action plan, on the group's individual and collective learning, and on the actions taken.	≈15 min.

Table 3.1 The CAL method's steps

Step 0

Topic preparation

Before going any further, let's see how Emilio prepares for the upcoming Codevelopment Action Learning (CAL) session (Figure 4.1). This is called Step 0.

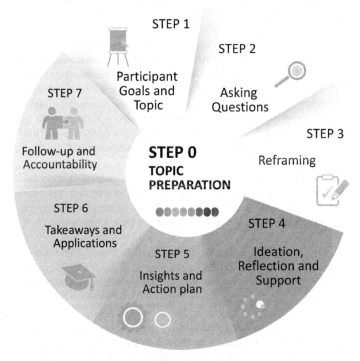

Figure 4.1 CAL's Step 0.

DOI: 10.4324/9781032625720-7

Step 0: topic preparation

It's a week before the first CAL session. Emilio has decided to be the client for this session and is eager to hear what his fellow directors have to say about the big challenge he will soon have to deal with, as he and his team of mostly new recruits tackle a major project. Barb, the facilitator, sends Emilio the topic preparation worksheet, to be completed before the first CAL session. She also arranges a 30-minute video call with him two days before the session, to discuss his goal and challenge that will become the learning topic for the group.

What topic can I bring to the group?

After a few days of reflection, Emilio finally figures out the topic he'll bring to the group's upcoming session.

He finds his new responsibilities somewhat daunting. To lead the construction of the new monorail, he must work with a team of first-level managers, most of whom are new hires and much younger than him.

> *Emilio asks himself: How can I get my team on board with the new project? They seemed comfortable with the subway upgrade, but that was a smaller project. At our last few sector meetings, they didn't seem thrilled with the prospect of building a monorail from scratch and go through the company's transformation. They'll need to work hard and put in plenty of overtime. What can I do to motivate them? The monorail has got to be a big success, it's a great opportunity to showcase our talent internationally!*

While Emilio's passion for change management is a great asset to the company, he needs to develop a different style to work with this new generation of managers. This is the challenge he decides to bring to the CAL group. This will become the learning topic for the group.

> *"OK, this idea is good enough, but how can I make it interesting for the others? What's the right way to present it? Barb, the facilitator, mentioned something about a Step 0. Better check that email she sent me a few days ago."*

After finding the email, Emilio fills out the CAL preparation worksheet as best as he can and sends it to Barb. It was difficult to find the right words, but Barb insisted at the kickoff meeting that he shouldn't spend too much time on the sheet.

> *"The Step 0 meeting with Barb will help clarify things, anyway,"* he thinks.

During their call, Barb tells Emilio that she has read and annotated his preparation sheet. She goes on to paraphrase her understanding of the topic. Then, to help Emilio clarify his ideas for the final version, she asks him a few questions. Here are two examples: (see later in this chapter for a more complete list)

- What have you already done to address the situation? How did that work out?
- Will this topic be a learning experience for the other participants? If so, how?

After the call, Emilio's thoughts are much clearer. The new wording for his topic is: "How can I align my team of leaders from different generations to get them on board for this major project? I'm looking for creative ideas and shared experiences." He amends his preparation sheet accordingly and writes down some notes about how he wants to present the topic in Step 1. Then, he sends it to Barb so she can email the topic to the group.

To generate even more insights, Barb also sends the participants a few articles on team motivation and change management.

Step 0 – objectives

The main objective of Step 0 is to help the client prepare their topic with the support of the facilitator before the CAL session.

Because CAL is about learning from each other by exploring an aspect of a participant's work-related activity, preparing the topic is a key step in the process.

What is a CAL topic?

Examples of CAL topics:

- A goal to be achieved
- A project to be fast-tracked
- An important decision to be made
- A challenge to be overcome

In Step 0, assisted by the facilitator, the client gets ready to present the essential facts of their topic and their needs to the group. This step also helps the client confirm their thoughts on their topic and confirms the topic's alignment with a variety of goals – their own, the groups, and those of the organization that's supporting the CAL process. The topic must also fall within the scope of the client's responsibilities, i.e., the client must be able to act on the topic and the situation. Finally, the topic must represent a learning opportunity, both for the client and the other participants. The facilitator plays a key role in helping the client meet these conditions.

A CAL topic must be:

- In your area of leadership and responsibility
- Important, serious, and concerning
- Current
- A resolvable issue, an objective, or an achievable project
- Concerns a situation that requires new solutions
- Encourages individual or organizational development
- A learning opportunity for the group

Facilitation tips – a CAL topic is not

- An organizational issue that falls outside the client's area of responsibility.
- An HR issue with legal ramifications that falls outside the CAL method's scope.
- A psychological issue or significant personal problem.
- A conflict or ethical dilemma between participants in the group.

For example, a CAL group for leaders might be formed to improve their change management skills. In this case, leaders will often bring topics such as: How can I mobilize my team around this change initiative? How can I have greater influence in this situation?

Another example: a CAL group for social workers to help give them more confidence and a new perspective on challenging cases.

Step 0 – benefits

Meaning and effect

By delivering a relevant, comprehensive, and concise topic, a successful Step 0 increases the session's effectiveness and improves participant satisfaction.

This is especially relevant for businesses that require the CAL group to produce clear results and measurable outcomes.

This phase can also bring to light possible confidentiality, ethical, or other sensitive issues with the topic so the client can decide how best to deal with them, thereby making the client feel more comfortable to propose their topic to the group and building trust with the facilitator.

Lastly, another part of Step 0 is that the agenda containing the overall theme of the CAL session is distributed to all participants, creating more interest and group engagement.

In some cases, the facilitator may wish to find relevant material, such as internal resources, articles, or videos, and send them to participants prior to the session.

Facilitating Step 0

The group uses a short CAL topic preparation worksheet to prepare Step 0 (see Appendix). The worksheet enables the participants to organize the materials that will be presented during Step 1 of the CAL group.

The worksheet is divided into two parts:

— Part 1 – Topic elements include: the title, key points (context, challenges, actions taken so far, impacts, plans, etc.), the desired outcome, and the type of group support the client wants.
— Part 2 – Learning: the topic's potential to be a learning opportunity for the client and the group, and the skills participants can develop by working on the topic.

The facilitator and the client also often set up a brief chat before the session, to finalize and validate the topic; see questions in the previous example or below.

Facilitation tips – what if Step 0 can't take place?

When a group has limited resources or preparation time, or when the intended client is absent, Step 0 can be accomplished by choosing another topic at the start of the session.

At the beginning of the session, the facilitator gives the group a few minutes to reflect, then asks each participant to come up with a potential topic. The group then decides which topic they want to address with the CAL method using two criteria: which participant has the greatest need to have their topic addressed, and which topic is most likely to be a learning opportunity for the whole group.

The facilitator asks the client a series of questions to help them fill out the CAL preparation worksheet. The goal is to help them be more efficient during Step 1 and feel more ready to open up in the group. Here are some examples (see the Appendix for more questions):

— Why is this topic important to you?
— Looking ahead 6–12 months, what do you think will have changed? What do you want to change?
— What have you already done to address the situation? How did that work out?
— What do you hope to achieve through the CAL session?
— How does your topic align with the group's theme?

–   Are there any potential confidentiality, ethics, or other sensitive issues? Are any participants involved or impacted by this topic?
–   Will this topic be as a learning experience for your fellow participants?
–   Can you give your topic a short title that would fit into a 280-character "tweet," for instance?
–   What leadership capabilities do you need to achieve your objective?

Step 0 – topic preparation

Main objectives

Organize ideas, summarize the topic's most important points, and express a precise need to the group. Identify the topic's relevance for the group.

Client's role

Choose a topic that directly affects them – a goal, project, decision, or challenge – and that provides learning opportunities for both the client and the group.
Decide what kind of support they want from the group: get new ideas from the consultants, brainstorming, reflect further, or another kind of assistance.
Fill out the CAL topic preparation worksheet.

The consultants are not called on during this step.

Facilitator's role

Review the preparation worksheet to ensure the topic is clearly expressed, the client's expectations are clear, the topic provides learning opportunities for other participants and is consistent with the group's theme.
Offer to help the client, where required. Check for any potential confidentiality, ethical or other sensitive issues.
Send participants the agenda for the session, including the subject line of the topic.
Where appropriate, send participants relevant additional resources to stimulate interest, get them thinking and spark ideas.
Suggested time: Max. 30 minutes for an email exchange and a brief discussion.
Tools: CAL topic preparation worksheet – Step 0; sample questions for the facilitator – Step 0 (see Appendix).

Table 4.1 Summary table for Step 0

Why have a Step 0?

From the point of view of improving performance and efficiency, and because CAL groups use organizational resources, the suggested topics must be aligned with the objective or strategic priority that was behind the group's implementation.[1]

Aligning objectives in this way also helps make the learning process more meaningful. According to the adult learning theory formulated by Malcolm Knowles, also known as andragogy,[2] experience and problem solving are more effective learning tools than simply transmitting content. As with other Action Learning schools of practice, CAL reflects this theory. Moreover, adults learn best by setting their own learning intentions, especially if these are directly related to their work or personal life. This is where CAL distinguishes itself from most other learning methods.

However, while crucial, Step 0 has not always been part of the ever-changing CAL method.

Payette and Champagne's first book[3] described Steps 1–6 of the original Codevelopment method, which represents the core of the sessions.

Three years later, Payette published a paper summarizing the Codevelopment method – with a twist: the value-added component was client preparation prior to Step 1, which the author said was both relevant and important for the client. He justified Step 0 by explaining that this preliminary stage takes place outside the session and doesn't involve the other participants.

Based on this idea, the authors of this book have described how to complete Step 0 in a previous book,[4] in the Coaching Ourselves Flash Codev module[5] and in training materials for facilitators.

Learning journal

In a few words, what is your key insight from this chapter (Step 0)?

After reading the last few chapters, has your opinion of CAL changed? If so, how?

What kind of topic would you like your organization to address with CAL?

References

1. Saks, A. M., & Haccoun, R. R. (2019) *Managing performance through training and development* (8th ed.). Nelson Education Ltd.
2. Knowles, M. S., Holton, E. F., & Swanson, R. A. (2015). *The adult learner: The definitive classic in adult education and human resource development* (8th ed.). Routledge.
3. Payette, A., & Champagne, C. (1997). *Le groupe de codéveloppement professionnel*. Presses de l'Université du Québec.
4. Sabourin, N., & Lefebvre, F. (2017). *Collaborer et agir: Mieux et autrement: Guide pratique pour implanter des groupes de codéveloppement professionnel*. Éditions Sabourin Lefebvre.
5. Coaching Ourselves. (2022). *Flash Codev: Accelerate goal achievement and consolidate competencies*. https://coachingourselves.com/modules/codevelopment/

Step 1

5

Participant goals and topic

Everybody has arrived (or is connected), participants have shared their latest news and checked in. It's time to start the Codevelopment Action Learning (CAL) session with Step 1 (Figure 5.1).

In this chapter, we cover this step's two main objectives: paving the way for learning and transformation by setting clear goals and focussing on the client's presentation of the topic.

Now, let's see how the facilitator, Barb, initiates Step 1.

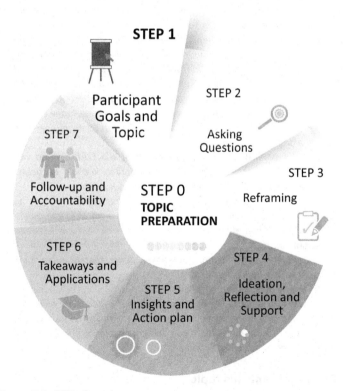

Figure 5.1 CAL's Step 1.

DOI: 10.4324/9781032625720-8

Step 1: participant goals and topic

It's 9 a.m. Barb (facilitator) and Emilio (client and Director, Engineering & Operations) are the first ones at the session. They greet the other participants as they arrive: Nat (Marketing), Ron (Finance), Gen (Supply Management), Ben (IT), and Max (HR-Communications). They're happy to have an opportunity to reconnect during this busy time. While they're catching up on personal and professional news, Barb makes sure that all the necessary material is available. After a few moments, she calls them to order: "So great to hear you laugh. Welcome! Time to begin, folks!"

Learning intentions

(Barb) *Greetings everyone. I'm happy to be here, and to be the CAL facilitator for our new group. We'll be using the CAL Method to learn from each other and build our abilities as leaders.* (Barb goes over the steps and the principles with the group.)

In summary, the theme of our session is: 'Align and motivate a team of leaders from different generations.' The key competencies we want to focus on are team leadership and how to promote engagement.

I suggest we focus on why we're here today and what we want to learn from each other.

Let's get started with Step 1. First, I'd like us to take two or three minutes to think about and write down our goal or learning intention for today. Then, we'll share them with the group. Your intention could be to learn the CAL method itself, or to develop skills that are useful in a CAL context, such as listening, questioning, and providing feedback and your reflective practice. It can also be about today's topic. This process of identifying your learning intentions will get easier as we go along, but let's give it a try.

(Short pause) (Nat) *Shall I go first? Well, the CAL method you talked about last time really piqued my interest. It could be useful with my team. So, I'd like to know more about it.*

(Ron) *Since my team is going through the same challenge as Emilio's, I want to learn about ways to improve my leadership with the new generation of leaders.*

(Gen) *You mentioned listening. Since I'm always the first to speak and I tend to be very... umm... outspoken during discussions, I think my goal would be to work on that.*

Everyone takes a turn speaking.

(Barb) (Goes last) *My goal is to practice my facilitation skills but also to learn about each one of you, to get to know everyone better. I'm excited to learn more about you and your projects. This is my first time working in the engineering sector.*

Emilio presents his topic

(Barb) *Now that the table is set and our goals are clear, are you ready to present your topic, Emilio? Please describe your topic and don't forget to tell us how the group can support you. You have five to ten minutes.*

(Emilio) All right. My topic concerns my new team for our new big project, the monorail. I have eight managers under me – all mechanical engineers. Two of them are in their forties. I know them, and we work well together.

For the next ten minutes, Emilio gives more details about his topic. He finishes with his goal and request for support.

(Emilio) My goal is to have a team of independent, motivated leaders who will work hard to complete this major project. And finally, here's what I need from the CAL group: I need the group to share their personal experiences aligning and motivating leaders from different generations, and maybe some tricks or techniques that worked for you. Help me figure out what I should do.

(Barb) Thanks, Emilio. Thanks for being our brave first client.

Step 1 – objectives

The two main objectives of Step 1 are: each participant must decide on their own goal and/or learning intention for the session. Next, the client must clearly present their topic and decide what kind of support they want from the group.

Step 1 – benefits

Identifying their learning goal

Identifying and sharing their goal or learning intention with the group helps create meaning for each participant. This is also when participants share what they want to get out of the session through mutual learning.

Communication and listening skills

Next, the client presents their topic. While you may think this would be a relatively simple task, it can in fact be quite tricky. Presenting a complex situation that affects them personally means honing their communication skills and their ability to summarize.

As for the consultants, Step 1 is an opportunity for them to practice their listening skills. In our fast-paced world, finding the focus for attentive listening can be a challenge. Haven't we all felt the urge, after three or four minutes, to jump in and ask a question, offer advice, or exclaim, "Wow, amazing! That's exactly what I'm going through now."?

Step 1 enables participants to practice their communication and listening skills – so important in today's world.

Facilitating Step 1

Participant goals/learning intentions

Because it can be difficult for participants to set a goal/learning intention for the first few sessions, the facilitator can remind them of the four main categories of goals/learning intentions that can be achieved through the CAL method[1]:

- Gain a deeper understanding of the topic, for example when consultants have a similar concern or are in the same situation.
- Develop skills related to the CAL method, such as active listening, asking questions, giving feedback, and reflective practice.
- Learn more about the CAL method.
- Depending on the theme, acquire a new skill or competency, such as political or leadership skills.

The facilitator can also hand out the CAL Think Sheet (see Appendix), which participants can use to record their learning intentions and take notes during the session.

Learning intentions – examples

- I want to improve my ability to ask more open-ended questions that make people think, rather than quickly responding with advice.
- I'm in the same situation as the client. I want to use what I learn from their topic to find ways to rapidly resolve the issue.
- I want to learn how to introduce the CAL method to my team.
- I want to feel more comfortable using strategies to stimulate creativity in my team.

See Part 4 for more examples of skills that can be developed using CAL.

Each participant can decide for themselves whether they want to keep their goal or learning intention for more than one session or set new ones for each session.

Writing down the participants' goals or learning intentions enables the facilitator to more effectively guide them through the steps, especially Steps 6 and 7, or from one session to the next. Rather than focussing exclusively on the client and their topic, the facilitator's action increases the potential for learning by all participants and applying that knowledge to their work.

Facilitation tips – dealing with reluctant participants

Some people find it difficult to adhere to CAL's highly structured yet flexible approach. Many of us are used to the "act first, think later" model of behaviour and are more accustomed to arguing and pushing our own point of view than asking questions about the other person's ideas. So, how can we deal with people who are reluctant to change their habits?

- At the start of each session, take the time to explain the steps, the expected outcomes, and legitimize the frustration people may feel at adhering to the structure, such as being asked to wait before proposing solutions.
- Ask the participant to be open to the method for this session, and ask if you can talk to them afterwards.

Talk to the participant after the session is over. Ask questions to help you understand where their reluctance is coming from. Does it express a need? Could CAL help them meet this need, or do they need to be supported in another way? Have they perhaps been pressured into attending?

Topic presentation

First, the client's presentation must be clear and concise, while still providing enough information so the consultants have a general understanding of the issue at hand.

When Step 0 is done before the session, the client's presentation generally takes about 10 minutes.

At the end of the presentation, the client's request for support must be clear. Do they want to share experiences? Get more thought-provoking questions? Hear possible solutions?

During the presentation, the consultants should listen carefully and attentively to the client. This isn't the time to interrupt, ask questions, or offer instant advice. To encourage focused listening, the facilitator can encourage participants to make notes on their Think Sheet.

In situations where Step 0 wasn't done, the client's request is often unclear. In that case, the facilitator can either ask the client to choose the kind of support they want or else to prioritize.

Facilitation tips – helping the client during the topic presentation

Even if the client prepared their topic in Step 0, they may have missed some important details. In such cases, the facilitator can prompt the client with a few questions:

— Can you tell us what actions/solutions you've tried so far?
— What are your desired outcomes and results?
— How can the group best support you?

Step 1 – Participant goals and topic

Main objectives

Briefly present the goals/learning intentions (all participants).
Summarize the topic (client).

Client's role

Present their goal and/or learning intention and listen to those of the group.
Present their topic to the group.
Explain what they want to achieve (their goal), and what kind of
support they want from the group.

Consultants' role

Present their goal and/or learning intention.
Listen to the client as they present their topic and take notes.
Focus on the client's desired outcome, the kind of support they want to
receive.

Facilitator's role

Present their goal and/or learning intention.
Ensure the client clearly states their expectations.
Ask the consultants to practice non-verbal active listening.

Suggested time: ≈20 min

Learning intentions: ≈10 min; presentation: ≈ 10 min

Tool: CAL Think Sheet – Seven steps (see Appendix)

Table 5.1 Summary table for Step 1

Goal setting and active listening

Goal setting

At the start of Step 1, the facilitator helps ensure that each participant's
goal or learning intention is specific and explicit, that it is both challenging and meaningful for the participant. In Steps 6 and 7, which
are designed to reinforce learning and action, the facilitator ensures
that the participant receives feedback on the progress they have made
towards that goal.

This practice is inspired by the four main principles of goal setting theory[2,3] and the appreciative inquiry approach.[4,5] When these theories are applied, the group is able to develop a positive attitude towards the future that promotes effective learning and helps create meaning and motivation for action among the participants. This increases the likelihood the group will generate positive impacts at the individual and organizational level.

Active listening

Active listening means giving your full attention to what others are saying. It means temporarily setting aside your own agenda and biases and assuming a non-judgemental attitude. CAL consultants must have the ability to see beyond the surface details of the client's story, so they can gain a deeper understanding of the client's experience, as opposed to giving free rein to their own thoughts or planning what they will say next.[6]

As noted by Marilee Adams, falling into a Judger Mindset can be a spontaneous, sometimes unconscious, response.[7] Because of this, when we actively listen and become aware that we're judging someone (their problem is their fault; what's wrong with them? etc.), it's time to step back for a moment and change our attitude to one of curiosity, where we focus on learning the facts and the client's experience. Having a Learner Mindset and being curious vastly improves the consultant's listening skills and enables them to ask better questions during Step 2.

Before getting to Step 2, the consultants can practice non-verbal active listening. They can be attentive by refraining from interrupting the client, by staying silent or by taking notes.[6] In our fast-paced, solution-oriented world, learning active listening skills represents a significant challenge.

Suggestions for further reading include the works of Locke and Latham, Cooperrider et al., Guffey et al., and Adams, which can be found in the "References" section.

Learning journal

In a few words, what is your key insight from this chapter (Step 1)?

How is a CAL group different from a problem-solving group?

After reading this chapter, how would you rate your own active listening skills? What could you improve?

References

1. Lafranchise, N. (2013). *Étude du cheminement des groupes de codéveloppement et des personnes participantes, dans le contexte d'un CSSS*. Université du Québec à Montréal.
2. Locke, E. A., & Latham, G. P. (2002). Building a practically useful theory of goal setting and task motivation: A 35-year odyssey. *American Psychologist, 57*(9), 705–717. https://doi.org/10.1037/0003-066X.57.9.705
3. Locke, E. A., & Latham, G. P. (1990). *A theory of goal setting & task performance*. Prentice Hall.
4. Cooperrider, D. L., Whitney, D., & Stavros, J. M. (2008). *Appreciative inquiry handbook: For leaders of change* (2nd ed.). Crown Custom.
5. Cooperrider, D. L., Zandee, D. P., Godwin, L. N., Avital, M., & Boland, B. (Eds.). (2013). *Organizational generativity: The appreciative inquiry summit and a scholarship of transformation* (1st ed.). Emerald.
6. Guffey, M. E., Loewy, D., & Griffin, E. (2019). *Business communication: Process & product*. Nelson Education.
7. Adams, M. G. (2022). *Change your questions, change your life: 10 powerful tools for life and work* (4th ed.). Berrett-Koehler Publishers.

Step 2

Asking questions

6

Reflecting promotes learning, new ideas, and change. Asking questions is a major part of the Codevelopment Action Learning (CAL) method (Figure 6.1).

The consultants will now dig deeper into Emilio's topic to help him open new possibilities. Let's see how the group manages to do so during Step 2.

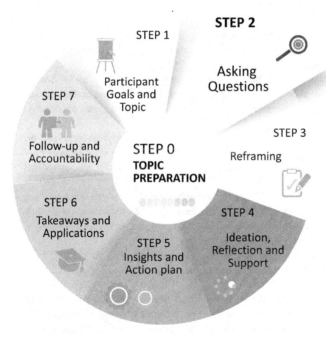

Figure 6.1 CAL's Step 2.

Step 2 – asking questions

(Barb) *Thanks, Emilio, for being our brave first client. I understand that you're looking for personal experiences and ideas that could help you align and motivate your new team. More specifically, you want strategies that work with younger individuals, who you're less used to interacting with.* (Emilio nods)

(Barb) *Okay folks. Let's get on with Step 2 – the asking questions phase. For the next 20 minutes or so, our job is to ask Emilio questions. Why? First, we'll ask questions so each of us has a better understanding of his topic. Second, we'll ask the kind of questions that make Emilio think, help him see his topic from a new angle so he can find his own solutions.*

Do any of you remember what our questions should focus on, to make them more useful and effective? You can refer to the "Sample powerful questions guide to help you."

(Gen) *Hmm… I think we should ask open-ended questions, if possible, so Emilio can think about his situation differently and explain it better. And I also remember that you told us we shouldn't hide suggestions in our questions, like, 'Have you tried such and such?'*

(Barb) *Exactly. If you have a great suggestion or experience to share with Emilio, please write it down and we'll get to it in Step 4. Anything else?*

(Max) *I remember reading on the sheet you gave us for Step 2 that we should try to ask questions about the context of the topic, or the person bringing the topic – in this case, Emilio – as opposed to just focusing on the topic itself.*

(Barb) *That's right. You can take turns asking questions until no one has anything left to ask. Emilio, all you have to do is answer. Feel free to tell us if ever you're not comfortable answering a particular question, that's totally okay.*

My role here is to listen and ask questions if we're stuck or if we stay too long on one type of question. And, remember: we're only looking for information and reflection now, not solutions. Is everyone ready? Okay, who wants to start?

(Ron) *You said you've got six new people on your team. How are those critical first stages of their projects going? Is everything on schedule?*

(Emilio) *Yes! We've been lucky: nobody got sick, the weather was perfect, we even had some extra pieces of heavy equipment, just in case, because Marc's team hasn't begun preparing the ground yet. But, honestly, with my previous team, at this point, we'd already be ahead of schedule! And, as you know, having a bit of wiggle room in your schedule is like money in the bank! We never know what we'll find once we start digging, there could be shipment delays for materials … But it feels like all my new team members can think about is having BBQs and going to their cottage, stuff like that…*

(Barb) *Anyone else?*

(Nat) (Raises her hand) *Besides our group, who else could support you find ways to deal with your new team?*

(Emilio) *What do you mean? Help me manage my team, or coach me?*

(Nat) *Either one. I'm just asking who else could support you. It's up to you to answer.* (Smiles)

(Emilio) (Thinks) *Good question! I hadn't thought about that. I could definitely ask Richard to do some coordinating – he's one of my two longest-serving team members. I could start by telling him about my challenge and ask him for his opinion. So far, he seems to get along fine with his new co-workers. Maybe he would take on a coordinating role but, if so, we'd have to change some of his responsibilities. Otherwise, our VPs are really overwhelmed with the project. I get along really well with Suzanne and Mathieu in HR, but apart from talking about it over lunch here and there, I'm not sure they can spare any time.*

(Ben) *Have you talked to your managers about your frustration, or your concerns regarding the project?*

(Emilio) *I haven't really talked to them about it yet, except to ask if the project is on schedule. I feel like, if I go there, it would end badly. I'm not even sure I'm the right person to do it. So, no, I haven't talked to them yet. That's why I'm here.*

(Max) *You say the VPs are too busy to get involved. Have you thought about asking them to give you some coaching support?*

(Barb) *OK, everyone, hold on a minute! Sorry to interrupt, Max, but my "special senses" are telling me that was a solution you just gave there! What do you think?*

(Max) (Laughs) *Totally, my bad! I think we're all kinda used to going straight to solutions. Sorry, Emilio. Pretend I never said anything.*

(Barb) *Your idea is fine, Max, but your timing is off. Write it down and tell us about it in Step 4. For now, how could you turn your potential solution into a question?*

(Max) *Ummm... What resources are available to help support your new team? I know it's not the same for all departments.*

(Barb) *Great!*

(Emilio) *I really feel like I need to talk to Suzanne about this. I have the same discretionary budget you all do. I wasn't told that I could use it for myself. I have this group, and that's pretty much it for now. Maybe I should call HR?*

(Barb) *Now that Ron, Nat, Ben, and Max have asked a question, it's your turn, Gen. I'll go after you.*

The group continues asking questions for another ten minutes.

Step 2 – objectives

Step 2 is where the CAL method starts to come into its own. Because it opens the door to new possibilities, many people consider this to be the most important step. This is where participants take the time to explore and reflect – actions that many of us neglect in our daily routine. By asking the client a series of questions, the group reflects on all of the components of Step 1 and gives the client a new perspective on their topic.

The consultants ask questions in order to gain insight into the client's reality and to ensure everyone has a clear understanding of the topic. The questions also enable the client to reflect on their own topic and think about possible solutions.

Step 2 – benefits

The art of effective questioning

One of CAL's most significant benefits is its role in creating a safe space where participants can practice a complementary skill to listening, i.e., the ability to ask thought-provoking questions that stimulate reflection and learning.

For leaders, learning how to ask the right kind of questions can make you a better coach[1]; for team members, asking questions can help strengthen relationships and improve teamwork.[2]

Yet, when someone tells you about a problem, what's the first thing you do?

Chances are, you might make suggestions, give advice, or offer ideas. Or maybe you ask a few questions to help you understand the situation. These are all natural reactions.

However, when the situation is more complex, asking open-ended, reflective questions makes it possible to explore different possibilities, learn from each other, and generate new ideas. Most importantly, this approach enables the person with the problem to come up with their own solutions, thereby increasing the likelihood they will act on their ideas and start a process of real change.

Facilitating step 2

Type of questions

On the face of it, asking questions may seem relatively simple and straightforward. This is true, but only partly so. In fact, asking questions in order to stimulate reflection and learning is a much more complex process.

In a CAL group, the facilitator encourages participants to ask questions that focus on three areas of interest: the topic itself; the context; and the client's actions, thoughts, and emotional experiences (see Figure 6.2 and sample questions, below).

The straightforward part of asking questions refers to the topic. Generally speaking, when dealing with a work-related issue or situation,

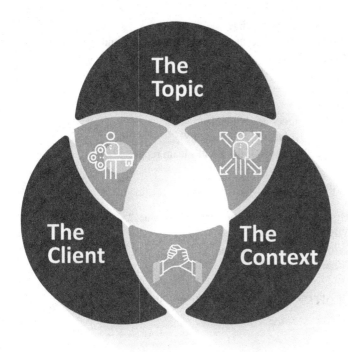

Figure 6.2 Three areas of interest for questionning.

team members readily ask questions so they can better understand or reflect on it. They also generally feel comfortable asking questions about the context. However, even though they're key to the reflective process, it's less common to talk about personal issues in a workplace context. It's important to take the client into account; this promotes greater awareness of their situation and experiences, as well as their own reactions, and so promotes learning.

Because CAL sessions are seen as a safe space, consultants can feel free to ask the client non-intrusive questions on issues that will help them move forward with their topic. If a consultant is thinking of asking a potentially sensitive question, they can ask the client if they would consent to answer such a question. If not, the client can simply reflect on it on their own.

Sample questions for consultants during Step 2.

The topic:

- You mentioned (…), can you tell us more about that?
- What have you been asked to do?
- If you could wave a magic wand and solve the problem, what would that look like?
- What risks would you potentially have to deal with?

- What is working? Why?
- What aspects of the situation can you control, and which ones can you not?

The context:

- What resources are available to you?
- Who is involved in the situation?
- Who do members of the client's team report to?

The client:

- How is this situation impacting your values?
- What makes you hesitate?
- Why is it important to you?
- What are your needs?

See the Appendix for more sample questions.

Facilitation tips – dealing with unresponsive or shy participants

CAL's success relies on collective intelligence. How can we deal with more reflective participants, the ones who are less comfortable speaking up in a group setting?

- Use open-ended questions that validate their experience, such as: *"The group hasn't heard your point of view yet. I know your insights would enrich our discussion. What do you think of the question that's just been asked?"*

Be mindful of peoples different learning styles by allowing time for reflection. *"Please take a moment now to think about questions that would help the client open up to new possibilities, or you can use the suggested questions in the available resources."*

An important rule

Throughout Step 2, participants are asked not to ask implicit suggestions. Consultants should ask open-ended questions like, "Other than you, who knows about this situation?" rather than ones that seem to endorse a certain course of action, such as: "Have you tried telling your colleagues about the situation?"

Focussing on open-ended questions counters our natural tendency to jump into action. By taking the time to step back, we gain greater clarity and deeper insight.

Facilitation tips – how to involve each consultant in Step 2?

We suggest consultants who are new to the CAL method take turns, each of them asking one question at a time. This way, everyone can participate and contribute to the client's reflection process. Also, the more minds at work, the greater the chances that the three areas of interest will be covered.

If the facilitator notices that the consultants are focussing on only one or two areas of interest, the facilitator can point that out, remind them of the kind of questions that should be asked, and emphasize the importance of covering all types of questions.

If a consultant does happen to make an implicit suggestion, it's not a big deal. The facilitator can simply ask them to turn the suggestion into a question and/or to write down the suggestion for Step 4. However, people who are new to CAL may be frustrated that the facilitator prevents them from moving on to suggestions immediately. To prevent this, we suggest that the facilitator remind people at the beginning of Step 2 that implicit suggestions will have to be rephrased.

Step 2 – Asking questions

Main objectives

Clarify the topic for the group and stimulate the client's reflection process.

Client's role

Listen and reflect.

Answer questions openly without justifying themselves.

Take notes.

Consultants' role

Ask questions about the topic; the context; and the client's actions, thoughts, and feelings to gain a clearer understanding and stimulate the client's thought process.

Keep their solutions for Step 4 (Ideation, reflection, and support).

Facilitator's role

Guide consultants to ask open-ended, reflective, or non-leading questions that encourage the client's thought process.

Where necessary, refocus the group or individual participants by asking a question from an area that's been omitted: the topic, context, or client.

Suggested time: ≈20 min

Tool: CAL think sheet – Seven steps; Sample powerful questions guide – Step 2 (see Appendix)

Table 6.1 Summary table for Step 2

The art of effective questioning

Asking questions is as much an art[3] as a science[4] and there are many books and videos on the topic.

We have used a number of approaches to asking questions (such as the Appreciative Inquiry[5] approach) as the basis for developing questioning tools that we use in our research and practice.

For example, David Clutterbuck, a coaching and mentoring consultant, asserts that the characteristics of a powerful question are as follows (the letters conveniently make the acronym PRAIRIE)[6]:

- Personal – it's about them, or about how they connect to an issue
- Resonant – it has an emotional impact
- Acute/ Incisive – it gets to the heart of the issue
- Reverberating – it stimulates reflection both in the moment and for some time afterwards
- Innocent – the intent of the questioner is not self-interested or derived from an agenda of their own
- Explicit – clearly and explicitly expressed.

Coach, facilitator, and speaker Marilee Adams recommends asking ourselves four questions – remembered by the acronym ABCD – as a way to move from a Judger to a Learner mindset. The questions illustrate the mental process behind the shift in focus; we have adapted the questions to better reflect CAL.[7]

- (Be) Aware – am I in a Judger mindset?
- Breathe – do I need to step back and reflect, to look at the situation more objectively?
- Curiosity – do I have all the facts? What's happening here?
- Decide – what's my choice? How can I support the client?

Hal Gregersen, former Executive Director of the MIT Leadership Center,[8,9] states that effective questions capture the listener's attention, arouse their curiosity, encourage creative thinking, create energy, and open up new possibilities. Importantly for CAL, a good question often leads to more questions.

Gregersen also suggests that a group will get better results by starting with factual, descriptive questions (what's working? what's not?, etc.), before moving on to more reflective, speculative questions (what if? what might be causing X?, etc.).

In short, Step 2 is the perfect setting in which to ask different kinds of questions, thereby developing your effective questioning skills, which will certainly be useful in other contexts.

You may also want to create your own list of questions based on the ones that worked for you, or by reading the works listed in the References section.

Learning journal

In a few words, what is your key insight from this chapter (Step 2)?

After reading this chapter, how would you rate your own questioning skills? What could you improve?

How can you encourage CAL group participants to be more curious?

References

1. Bungay Stanier, M. (2016). *The coaching habit: Say less, ask more & change the way you lead forever*. Box of Crayons Press.
2. Schein, E. H. (2013). *Humble inquiry: The gentle art of asking instead of telling*. Berrett-Koehler Publishers, Inc.
3. Vogt, E. E., Brown, J., & Isaacs, D. (2003). *The art of powerful questions: Catalyzing, insight, innovation, and action*. Whole Systems Associates; Pegasus Communications.
4. Schaeffer, N. C., & Presser, S. (2003). The science of asking questions. *Annual Review of Sociology, 29*(1), 65–88. https://doi.org/10.1146/annurev.soc.29.110702.110112
5. Cooperrider, D. L., Whitney, D., & Stavros, J. M. (2008). *Appreciative inquiry handbook: for leaders of change* (2nd ed.). Crown Custom.
6. Clutterbuck, D. (2013). *Powerful questions for coaches and mentors: A practical guide for coaches and mentors*. Wordscapes.
7. Adams, M. G. (2022). *Change your questions, change your life: 10 powerful tools for life and work* (4th ed.). Berrett-Koehler Publishers.

8. Gregersen, H. B. (2018). *Questions are the answer: A breakthrough approach to your most vexing problems at work and in life.* HarperCollins Publishers.
9. Gregersen, H. B. (2018). Better brainstorming: Focus on questions, not answers, for breakthrough insights. *Harvard Business Review*, March/April, 64–71.

Step 3

7

Reframing

People often jump into action without taking the time to think about the situation. In this chapter, we'll go through Step 3. This is the step where first the consultants and then the client reframe the topic, before the group moves on to talking about action and solutions (Figure 7.1).

Figure 7.1 CAL's Step 3.

DOI: 10.4324/9781032625720-10

Step 3: reframing

(Barb) *Now that everyone has asked their questions, I think we're ready for Step 3. There are two components to this step. In the first half, the consultants take two minutes to think about what they've just heard, then they'll write down their understanding of Emilio's topic. Then, you'll take turns sharing your understanding of his topic, goal, and request for support. To promote positive communication, think about beginning your sentences with words like:*

- *I understand...*
- *I hear...*
- *I feel...*
- *I wonder...*

Afterward, in the second half of the step, Emilio will use the consultants' insights to reframe his topic and tell us how we can best support him in Step 4. Let's take two minutes to collect our thoughts. Please let me know when you're ready to move on.

First half: reframing by the consultants

(Gen) *I'll start.*

(Barb) *Are you sure? I remember you told us that your goal today was to practice listening, instead of going first. Do you still want to practice that skill?* (Smiles)

(Gen) *Hah, you're right! How about we start with Ben then?* (Nudges Ben, sitting next to her.)

(Ben) *Okay, why not? I understand that your team has new members, and that six of them are millennials. I also understand that you have good chemistry with them, but that you're puzzled by some of their attitudes, towards the project or just in general. For instance, one of them didn't answer his phone on the weekend, when the excavation team was doing critical work and needed his input. For him, it wasn't a big deal but, for you, it is.*

Since you don't have any children or friends in that age group, you told us you feel a bit on your back foot because it's not the same kind of interaction as with your previous team. So, your goal is to motivate them and improve the way you manage them. You asked us to share our experiences with people from that generation, what worked with them and what didn't, and offer a few suggestions.

(Barb) *Who's next? We'll finish with Gen.*

(Ron) *I agree with Ben, but I'd like to add something. My feeling: in order to continue being a top-notch director, to get everyone behind the common goal of building the monorail, you need to find out what makes you uncomfortable with your new team members. To help you figure that out, you want us to share experiences and how we've dealt with similar younger leaders in the past.*

(Nat) *I wonder if you need to find a better way of communicating with them. If you all understood each other better, you'd feel more comfortable communicating your expectations and motivating them. My understanding is that you want strategies that will help you figure out how to understand and interact with the younger members of your team.*

The other group members share their understanding of Emilio's topic. Then, Barb concludes by giving her own summary.

(Barb) *Thanks, everyone. Now, it's time to take a break. Emilio, please think about what the others shared. When we return, I want you to comment on what they said. Was their understanding of your topic correct? Or do you need to give us some more details? After that, we'll ask you to reframe your request for support. Based on what you told us in Step 1 and what we shared in Step 2, what is your goal, and how can the group help you reach that goal?*

Second half: reframing by the client

The group gets back together.

(Emilio) *First, I'd like to thank you all for listening to my story. The thoughts you shared afterwards showed you'd been listening carefully, and the way your reframed my topic was spot on! Yes, you're right: I <u>do</u> want to find a way to be a better leader for my younger team. That's still my goal. However, what Ron said struck a chord. I still want you to share your experiences and give me ideas about what to do. But, I'd also like you to help me find out what is making me uncomfortable when I interact with them. That way, I'll be able to do something about it.*

(Barb) *Great. Now, we know what we need to focus on in Step 4.*

Step 3 – objectives

The main objective of Step 3 is to help the group take a step back, briefly reframe the client's topic, and request for support, before exploring solutions and moving on to action in Steps 4 and 5.

The consultants take turns sharing their understanding of the topic and the type of support requested. At this stage, the client doesn't respond; rather, they listen to the different perspectives and take notes to help them better understand the various aspects of their topic and their request for support. They can then move on and reframe their goal and request, if they want.

Because of the insights generated by the reframing process, this is a good time for the client to consider new ways of approaching their topic. Now that questions have been asked (Step 2) and the topic has been reframed (Step 3), the client's understanding of their topic will almost certainly have evolved.

At the end of Step 3, the client should therefore be able to clarify their goal and request for support to the group, in preparation for Step 4.

Step 3 – benefits

Providing supportive feedback

Step 3 is a time of openness and listening to different points of view, when all the consultants share how they see the situation. This is a great opportunity for the client to start developing their reflective thinking, through a process known as "divergent thinking." We'll discuss this concept in greater detail in Step 4.

At this stage, the consultants continue practicing effective communication. They provide the client with supportive, empathetic feedback using skills such as rephrasing and mirroring.

As for the client, they need to use active listening in order to be open to hearing perspectives that may differ from their own.

Facilitating Step 3

Reframing by consultants (first half)

In Step 3, the facilitator gives the group a few extra minutes so the consultants can write a few sentences that summarize their understanding of the topic. The summary should include the most important aspects of the topic (the topic itself, the context, and the personal aspects), the client's goal, and their request for support.

Consultants are encouraged to start their reframing with the following "I" statements, to promote positive communication:

- I understand ...
- I hear ...
- I feel ...
- I wonder ...

The consultants take turns sharing their understanding of the topic. Even if most aspects of the topic have already been covered, the consultants are still encouraged to summarize it in their own words. The more viewpoints, the greater the chance the client will gain new insights into their topic and see new ways of taking action.

If the topic is simple, the group is large, or time is short, the facilitator can ask only two or three consultants to share their insights.

Facilitation tips – helping the client during Step 3 (first half)

At the beginning of Step 3, the facilitator should remind the group that this step is about listening and being open to new perspectives. They should also ask the consultants to bear in mind that clients are sometimes uncomfortable with this step. Having their topic reframed by others, and listening to the shared points of view requires openness and humility on the part of the client, so consultants must be sensitive when sharing their thoughts.

We also suggest reminding the client that although they may be uncomfortable with the new perspectives they hear, they are not obliged to accept them. Ultimately, they choose what they take away from the group.

Reframing by the client (second half)

In the last part of Step 3, the client is asked to reframe their topic and goal.

Even if they've done Step 0, at this point, the client has still had only one perspective on their topic. After summarizing the topic (Step 1), exploring the topic by answering questions (Step 2) and gaining insights into the consultants' perspectives (Step 3), the client may now be able to see new ways of approaching their topic, and possibly reframing their request for support. See Exhibit 2.5 (above) for an example of this.

Also, especially when Step 0 has not been done, some clients ask the group for several kinds of support. If this is the case, Step 3 is a good time to prioritize one of the requests, so it can be addressed in Step 4.

If the client decides not to change their initial request from Step 1, that's perfectly fine. The important thing is that the client feels free to change their request and doesn't feel obliged to stick with the original one. If they choose not to change it, Step 3 is simply shorter and there's more time for the rest of the session.

Facilitation tips – dealing with an indecisive client (second half)

In the first half of Step 3, after the consultants have shared their view of what they feel the client's situation and need is, the client may have trouble rephrasing their learning goal and request for support from the group, or they may not be able to decide on just one.

   –   Take a break after the consultants have reframed the topic. The facilitator can gently point out to the client that having multiple needs only confuses the other participants, and help them clarify their need.

To help the client reframe, the facilitator can help them prioritize by asking open-ended questions: "*In your reframing, I hear two different ideas (or requests for support). Which one would you like to pursue? Which one would be most useful in helping you achieve the learning goal that you mentioned in Step 1?*" (The facilitator names the goal.)

Step 3 – Reframing

Main objectives

Stimulates reflection on the topic and openness to new perspectives. Reframing must include the client's goal and their request for support from the group.

Client's role

Listen to the consultants reframe the topic (first half).
Decide on the desired outcome, tell the other participants what kind of support they want: experiences, ideas, more questions, food for thought, or practical support (second half).

Consultants' role

Everyone takes a few minutes to write down their understanding of (i.e., how they reframe) the topic (first half).
Take turns briefly articulating their understanding of the topic (using "I" statements to promote positive communication) and the client's request for support and their goal. Emphasize the topic's important aspects but be sure not to offer advice or solutions (first half).
Listen to the client's reframed topic (second half).

Facilitator's role

Ask the consultants to write down their understanding of the topic, the client's request for support and goal, then encourage them to share it (first half).
Help the client reframe their topic. Ask the client to write down their new subject line and/or request to the group (second half).
If necessary, encourage consultants to take a quick break or discuss what they have learned so far during the session to let the client review their new perspectives (second half).

Step 3 – (*Continued*)

Before moving on to Step 4, check that there is a common understanding of the topic and the client's request for support, especially if it has changed (second half).

Suggested time: ≈15 min

Tool: CAL think sheet – Seven steps (see Appendix).

Table 7.1 Summary table for Step 3

Providing social support through active listening and supportive feedback

In addition to opening new perspectives for the client, why is it so important to take the time to step back in Step 3?

By using supportive feedback to articulate their understanding of the topic, the consultants show the client that they have really listened to them.[1] This also shows that their situation is taken seriously and is important to the group. This is the group's way of acting on its offer of social support.

Because much has been written about social support in the workplace, there are many different definitions. Jolly et al. recently published an integrative review in the *Journal of Organizational Behavior* that gives the following definition:

> In general, social support refers to psychological or material resources that are provided to a focal individual by partners in some form of social relationship. These resources may have direct positive effects on important outcomes, such as the development of, or improvement in the quality of, social exchange relationships and job attitudes, or they may serve a buffering role between environmental stressors and an individual's appraisal of stress and/or experience of strain.
>
> (p. 229)[2]

Reframing the client's topic through supportive feedback closes the circle started in Steps 1 and 2 with active listening and asking questions, respectively.

In Step 5, we'll see that, in order to help participants take action and learn in a meaningful way, it's important to build their confidence and motivate them to engage with the process. This is one of the main reasons why the other participants provide social support through active listening.

Learning journal

In a few words, what is your key insight from this chapter (Step 3)?

What might the negative impacts be of omitting or hurrying through Step 3?

What potential roadblocks might the group run into when attempting to reframe the client's goal and topic? What would you do?

References

1. Guffey, M. E., Loewy, D., & Griffin, E. (2019). *Business communication: Process & product*. Nelson Education.
2. Jolly, P. M., Kong, D. T., & Kim, K. Y. (2021). Social support at work: An integrative review. *Journal of Organizational Behavior, 42*(2), 229–251. https://doi.org/10/ghd3tt

Step 4

Ideation, reflection, and support

8

Now that everyone has a good understanding of the client's reframed topic, it's time for the group to offer different kinds of ideas, reflection, and support. Let's see how it goes for Emilio's group during Step 4 (Figure 8.1).

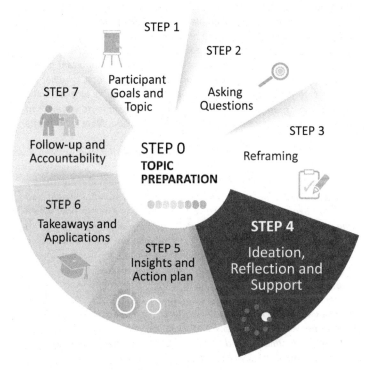

Figure 8.1 CAL's Step 4.

DOI: 10.4324/9781032625720-11

Step 4: ideation, reflection, and support

(Barb) (Looks at Emilio.) *As I understand it, you want some strategies to help you lead the younger members of your team. Also, you'd like the group to share their personal experiences and ideas on how to deal with the discomfort you're feeling. You'd also appreciate some reflective questions that will help you explore why you feel that way.*

(Emilio) *Exactly.* (Emilio gives the group a thumbs-up.)

(Barb) *Consultants, now it's your turn to share your ideas, experiences, and questions. You can also offer support to Emilio after the session. It's important to listen to each other, as you might be able to apply the ideas that others put forward to your own leadership practice.*

As for you, Emilio, at this point, I'd like to ask you to just listen and take notes. We recommend abiding by this guideline because, when we're reacting, we're not listening, and you might miss something really useful. Look at it this way: it's like we're presenting our thoughts to you on a silver platter. You'll have an opportunity to choose the ones that make the most sense to you in Step 5.

I suggest the consultants do as we did in Step 2: take turns sharing one idea or experience at a time. The most important guideline is that we must not judge anyone else's suggestions, whether we agree with them or not. At this point, our main goal is to give Emilio different perspectives, so he thinks about his topic in new ways and come up with different possible courses of action. Now, who wants to go first?

(Max) *Might as well be me, since I jumped the gun in Step 2.* (Laughs)

I think getting another perspective would help Emilio identify some habits he has, some ways of thinking and acting. It would also help us explore how he reacts to new situations like this one, where he's leading a team that's very different from anything he's had to deal with in the past. My situation is a bit different, but I've had some coaching to help me become a better leader too, for two employees who were on the autism spectrum. I really wanted to see things from their point of view and respect their differences. And, as HR Director, I think learning about diversity is part of my role. After all, our employees come from all over the world. So, I hired a diversity coach who specializes in diversity and inclusion. She helped me change some of my attitudes and she also taught me how to communicate my boundaries. I know it's not quite the same thing, as your managers aren't that different from you but still … different generations don't always see eye to eye.

(Ron) *Since you're not supposed to answer, Emilio, I'll jump in with a question!* (Laughs) *We're all overwhelmed with this project, we're very focused on the task at hand. And, you say you want to motivate and inspire your managers. I'm sure you know as well as I do that, when you want to mobilize your team, you need to appeal to their interests and values. So, going back to square one: do you know them? You've been working together for months now. What's stopping you from spending some time getting to know them?*

(Nat) *I'm going to start with an idea and follow it up with an offer of support. Emilio. I think we could reasonably ask our VPs if we could use some of our budget for coaching. You could ask just for yourself, but I'm pretty sure that a number of us would take advantage of the coaching if it was offered. We have Barb and the CAL group, but there are so many changes we must adapt to, we can't possibly address all the issues here. So, if you like, I'm offering to go with you and speak to one of the VPs. They'll be more likely to listen if we go together.*

(Gen) *In Purchasing, my management team has stayed the same but, lately, we've hired so many new warehouse workers that I suggested we organize a weekend of outdoor activities so everyone can get to know each other. I'm not sure that's exactly what you need – maybe an off-site strategic retreat? You'd need an excuse to get to know them better, but surely there's something you can do in the meantime? I hear the communication plan for the project's next phases isn't finalized yet. If you reviewed your team's roles and objectives based on this quarter's experience, you'd have a better idea of their interests and could adjust accordingly.*

The other participants, including Barb, suggest other ideas, share experiences, give possible solutions, and offer support.

(Barb) *Since we've heard everyone's suggestions, I think we can move on.*

(Emilio) *Oh boy, that gave me a lot to think about! Thanks a lot, everyone.*

(Barb) *Great! Now you're ready for Step 5.* (Smiles)

Step 4 – objectives

The main objective of Step 4 is to help the client achieve their goal by having the consultants share their experiences, ideas, possible solutions, and resources, as well as their own past experiences that could help the client decide on a course of action. This is also when the consultants go back to asking questions, to help the client move ahead in their thinking or possibly to offer practical support between sessions.

In order to offer the right kind of support, the consultants must have been listening attentively in Step 3, in case the client changes their request for support.

Another objective of Step 4 is that the consultants and facilitator also benefit by gaining insights or actionable ideas they can apply to their own work. This is the strength of mutual learning!

Step 4 – benefits

Creativity and co-created solutions

Step 4 is a dynamic and creative part of the Codevelopment Action Learning (CAL) process. Participants are usually happy they can finally share their ideas and experience in an open environment. The client remains silent and doesn't comment on what's shared; now, it's their turn to practice active listening.

At this stage, all ideas have equal merit, with no winners or losers. Instead, participants co-create solutions using collective intelligence, building on each other's ideas and sharing their experiences.

Participants learn how divergent thinking[1] can be used to generate new ideas and move projects and goals forward more quickly.

Facilitating Step 4

Two guidelines

First, the client is asked not to speak or react to the consultants' suggestions; just remain open, listen actively, and take notes (subsequently called the "Keep silent" guideline).

While this lack of discussion can feel unnatural at first, the idea behind this guideline is to keep the client in an open frame of mind. When we react or justify ourselves, by using phrases like, "I don't think it'll work," or "I'm not sure I can do that," we tend to be less receptive to new perspectives.

Asking the client to remain silent leads to more and more focused listening, something we often forget to do when we're involved in a heated debate. This also encourages more diverse and daring thinking.

No matter how outrageous they are, regardless of whether or not they failed in the past or in another context, these ideas may contain a potentially helpful kernel of truth. Also, no matter what the consultants suggest, the client has complete control over what's included in their action plan, to be developed in Step 5.

Facilitation tips – use "and" instead of "but"

We recommend the consultants take turns giving their point of view, followed by the facilitator, whose objective is to put forward ideas that haven't yet been expressed, or to kickstart the discussion, if necessary.

To stimulate co-creation, participants are asked to use the word "and" instead of "but."

If ideas are in short supply, the facilitator can break the group up into smaller groups of two or three to brainstorm. This often re-energizes the group and leads to more creative thinking.

Second, the consultants are asked not to argue or debate among themselves about the best solution, nor try to reach a consensus (subsequently called the "No Comment" guideline).

The goal of this guideline is to ensure a lively, no-holds-barred discussion that provides the client with new ideas and learning opportunities for everyone else. Because nothing is off limits, consultants throw out a wide variety of ideas. Likewise, because their ideas can't be debated, they are less likely to worry about being judged. By the same token, the resulting creative, out-of-the-box solutions are more likely to encourage everyone to come up with original, innovative actions.

To achieve this, consultants are asked not to comment on what any of the other consultants say, whether they agree with it or not. It's a good idea to remind everyone of these guidelines at the start of Step 4, so they aren't surprised if the facilitator has to cut off their discussion.

Step 4 – Ideation, reflection, and support

Main objectives

Help the client find new ways of seeing and thinking about their topic and offer support.

Client's role

Be open, listen silently and attentively to all the consultants' ideas; abide by the Keep Silent guideline.

Write down all suggested thoughts and action items, the consultants' questions, and receive the consultants' practical support.

During the optional short break, begin sorting the ideas for their action plan (see Step 5).

Consultants' role

Share ideas and thoughts with the client and offer practical support after the session is over.

Avoid arguing with other consultants; don't try and reach a consensus; abide by the No Comment guideline.

Write down any ideas that could be applied to their own situation.

During the optional short break, help the client sort out the ideas for their action plan (see Step 5).

Facilitator's role

Make sure the client is listening attentively.

Encourage consultants to express a variety of ideas, without arguing.

After the consultants have spoken, share your own ideas and reflections, to stimulate the discussion.

(Continued)

Step 4 – Ideation, reflection, and support

Where necessary, summarize and rephrase remarks. Ensure participants abide by the guidelines.

Encourage consultants to write down all the ideas. Do the same in preparation of future summary reports to participants.

During the optional short break, help the client sort out the ideas for their action plan (see Step 5).

Suggested time: ≈20 min + ≈5 min (optional break)

Tool: CAL think sheet – Seven steps (see Appendix)

Note: Just before Step 5 could be a good time to take a short break, for the client to review the suggested material.

Table 8.1 Summary table for Step 4

Facilitation tips – dealing with a person who dominates the conversation

- Avoid making eye contact with that participant. Instead, look at the other group members.
- If the group didn't agree on the order of speaking, ask people to take turns suggesting a course of action or talking about their experience, max. two or three minutes per person.
- If someone talks non-stop, you shouldn't hesitate to politely interrupt by asking them to briefly summarize their point. Point out that, for the CAL approach to be effective, you need input from a variety of perspectives, which means everyone should be given a chance to speak. The group expects you, as the facilitator, to chair the meeting well, including allocating speaking time. This is your job!

Ideation and divergent thinking

Step 4 represents one of the major departures from traditional Action Learning.[2] Here, the consultants and facilitator go beyond asking thought-provoking questions to sharing real-life experiences and suggesting possible solutions, which the client can include in their action plan.

During a regular discussion, people sometimes make negative comments about the ideas expressed by others. Because this can impact the group's creativity, these kinds of comments are discouraged in a CAL session. The No Comment guideline is based on one of the ways to stimulate divergent thinking[1,3] first proposed in the 1950s by psychologist J.P. Guilford. He stated that divergent thinking – a must for creativity – typically occurs during spontaneous, free-flowing, non-linear activities. Many ideas are generated, and many possible solutions are explored in a short amount of time. This approach is particularly useful in work settings, when new projects are being launched or when innovative solutions are required.

The creative ideation in Step 4 is followed by a complementary process in Step 5, in which the client uses convergent thinking to organize the ideas and information they have received as they create their action plan.

The No Comment guideline has yet another advantage for leaders and senior professionals. These kinds of people are used to pro-moting their ideas at work; they tend to try and "win" by having their ideas or solutions chosen. Anyone who disagrees with them is auto-matically wrong. These assumptions are behind the Model 1 stance described by Chris Argyris and Donald Schön, more recently labelled the Unilateral Control Model by Roger Schwartz.[4–6]

The authors argue that, if these same leaders act in accordance with the Model 2 stance, also called the Mutual Learning Model,[4–6] they are more collaborative, more effective, and more open to learning.

Leaders who adopt Model 2 are able to tolerate ambiguity and handle ideas and emotions that differ from their own. Rather than trying to be right at all costs, their starting point is that they could be wrong, so they try to gather as much relevant information as possible. They are also willing to listen to all ideas, even ones that people are hesitant to express, and use different points of view as learning opportunities.

However, theorists and practitioners alike agree that switching from the Unilateral to the Mutual Learning Model takes a great deal of practice, making the CAL session's divergent thinking exercise a good way to start acquiring this skill.

Learning journal

In a few words, what is your key insight from this chapter (Step 4)?

What facilitation techniques could you use in Step 4 to stimulate the participants' creativity and help them be more supportive?

What is your organization's attitude on the issue of debate (oppositional) versus dialogue (collaborative) and divergent thinking?

References

1. Runco, M. A. (2011). Divergent thinking. In M. A. Runco & S. R. Pritzker (Eds.), *Encyclopedia of creativity* (2nd ed., Vol. 1, pp. 400-403). Elsevier.
2. Paquet, M., Sabourin, N., Lafranchise, N., Cheshire, R., & Pelbois, J. (2022). Codevelopment Action Learning during the pandemic – findings from two online co-learning and co-creation events: Twenty Codevelopment Action Learning sessions were held simultaneously for 148 participants from nine French-speaking countries. *Action Learning: Research and Practice, 19*(1), 19–32. https://doi.org/10.1080/14767333.2022.2026761
3. Runco, M. A. (2014). *Creativity: Theories and themes: Research, development, and practice* (2nd ed.). Elsevier.
4. Argyris, C., & Schön, D. A. (1974). *Theory in practice: Increasing professional effectiveness*. Jossey-Bass.
5. Schwarz, R. M., Davidson, A. S., Carlson, M. S., & McKinney, S. C. (2005). *The skilled facilitator fieldbook: Tips, tools, and tested methods for consultants, facilitators, managers, and coaches* (1st ed.). Jossey-Bass.
6. Schwarz, R. M. (2017). *The skilled facilitator: A comprehensive resource for consultants, facilitators, coaches, and trainers* (3rd ed.). Jossey-Bass.

Step 5

Insights and action plan

9

Having the participants commit to taking action is a key component of Codevelopment Action Learning (CAL), one that distinguishes this approach from other kinds of group discussion (Figure 9.1).

Has the group succeeded in providing Emilio with food for thought and inspiring him to move forward? Let's see the development of his action plan.

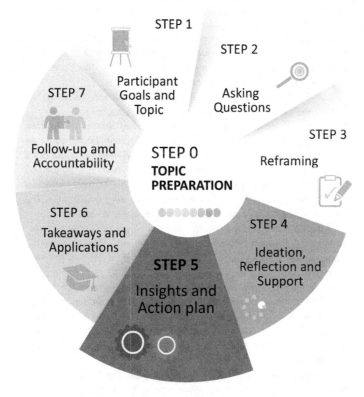

Figure 9.1 CAL's Step 5.

DOI: 10.4324/9781032625720-12

Step 5: insights and action plan

(Barb) *Congratulation, everyone! Step 4 was a big success, and Emilio has ended up with a pretty good list of ideas. To help him mull over what he just heard, I suggest we take a five-minute reflection time. Emilio, I'd like you to use the time to shift through the suggestions and choose the one that suits you best. Then, in Step 5, you'll tell us what you plan to do.*

Consultants, please review the ideas you noted and select the ones that you can integrate in your own situation.

(Five minutes later...)

(Emilio) *I'm ready, Barb. Thanks again, everyone, for your suggestions. I think my way forward is clear now.*

(Barb) *Great! So, tell us about your action plan. Be sure to say what the short-term actions are, and what you plan to do later. Also, I ask you not to comment on the suggestions you left out. We don't need to know why you didn't choose them. Just focus on what resonated with you, and what you plan to do.*

Consultants, we have to realize that Emilio might not choose our idea. While this may be a bit frustrating, remember that Emilio knows his own situation best, so he's the one who has to decide if a suggestion aligns with his circumstances, his experience, his personality, etc. And remember: an idea that gets passed over today might make more sense to him in the future, or perhaps another consultant will pick it up. Emilio, ready when you are.

(Emilio) *Well, first, thanks again for all these ideas. I already feel lighter, and I haven't even done anything yet.* (Laughs)

There are two things I plan to try in the next few days. As Ben suggested, I'll talk to my VP and see if coaching could count as part of my training budget. The coaching would help me figure out a better way to react when they say no to me or when I feel they aren't up to speed working hard enough. Ask more questions – where is their response coming from? – instead of reacting emotionally. The coach could also help me explore why I get angry so quickly.

Also, I clearly need to know them better. How can I figure out what motivates them if I'm only focusing on the project? This is not my old team, so I can't just do more of the same. This is so basic ... but easy to forget. So, thanks to Nat for that suggestion. I'll organize a short strategic retreat for my department, and include some social activities.

Last but not least, we could use the retreat to create a communication plan for the entire management team that would make it easier to pass on information and communicate priorities. The plan would also be an opportunity for me to clarify my expectations to my management team.

(Barb) *Thanks for sharing your action plan, Emilio. I'm glad you have some insights that you can act on in the near future. As you know, there's a Step 7 that we'll go through at the end of our next session. Is it okay with you if we follow up then about what you achieved in the meantime?*

(Emilio) *Of course. But I won't be able to get to everything on the list.*

(Barb) *That's okay. No need to rush. You can talk about what you got done and what's left to do. And we can also assess the group's progress over several sessions.*

(Emilio) *Fine with me.*

Step 5 – objectives

Step 5 may seem straightforward, but it's a crucial component of taking action. As previously mentioned, when assuming the client role, each participant must commit to moving beyond discussion, applying the action items from Step 4 and returning to the group with their results and what they learned. The objective of Step 5 is for the client to establish an action plan outlining what they will do after the session.

This is when the client explores what they have learned from Step 4 and chooses what makes sense for them and for their work. It's when they make a commitment to the group and to themself to take a first step to accelerate their goals and projects.

What are the short- and medium-term achievable actions they could take? What strengths and resources could be used to improve the likelihood of success? What will help the client to make progress towards their goal? What will make a real difference?

The client must also tell the other participants when – at the next session? the one thereafter? – they will share their progress with the group (Step 7).

Step 5 – benefits

Action and self-efficacy

The power of Step 5 lies in the client's newfound self-confidence, motivation, and empowerment.

At this point, the client feels supported in their actions, and this gives them the courage to act and move forward. Step 5 is the first step where participants are encouraged to see new ways of taking action, in order to feel more effective at work.

Facilitating Step 5

Facilitating Step 5 is usually quite straightforward. The client is asked to share their action plan and any key points that will guide their post-session thinking.

If the client simply reads through the suggestions from Step 4, the facilitator can ask a few questions to encourage convergent thinking and help the client organize their ideas. For example, the facilitator can ask the client to prioritize the suggestions, or choose which one(s) they think it's possible to implement.

"No Comment" guideline again in effect

To help participants feel free to bring a range of ideas to subsequent sessions, the client is asked not to judge the suggestions, questions, or support offered by the consultants, especially the ones that aren't chosen. This kind of non-judgemental attitude helps everyone feel safe. More specifically, it prevents consultants from feeling put down or belittled, which would hinder their active participation and the development of collective intelligence.

Similarly, the facilitator should remind the consultants that their ideas may not be chosen. If this is the case, arguing is not allowed. It's up to the client to decide which ideas are relevant for them. The facilitator can also point out that the ideas that aren't chosen might be useful at some point in the future, or used by another participant.

Facilitation tips – reflection time

Between Step 4 and Step 5, the facilitator can suggest the client take some time to reflect. The client can use this time to sort through and prioritize their options and decide whether the actions are immediate, short- or medium-term.

As for consultants, they can use this time to review the actions proposed in Step 4 and identify the ones that apply to their own situation. This way, each topic brought to the group can be a meaningful learning experience for everyone. Also, they can further help the client develop their action plan and prioritize their actions.

Step 5 – Insights and action plan

Main objectives

Identify concrete, short- and medium-term, achievable actions.

Client's role

Sort through the results of Step 4 and develop a preliminary action plan for themselves.

Make a commitment to the group to take action and move forward.

(Continued)

Consultants' role

Review the ideas from Step 4 during the reflection period.

Be non-judgemental about the client's chosen solutions.

If necessary, further help the client develop their action plan and prioritize their actions.

Facilitator's role

Ask the client to summarize which ideas they choose to keep in their action plan.

Guide the client in prioritizing their actions.

Write down the client's action plan in preparation for Step 7.

Suggested time: ≈10 min

Tool: CAL think sheet – Seven steps (see Appendix)

Table 9.1 Summary table for Step 5

CAL and self-efficacy

Psychologist Albert Bandura is the originator of both social cognitive theory and the concept of self-efficacy.[1]

Simply put, self-efficacy refers to a person's belief in their ability to execute behaviours and accomplish tasks.[2] Self-efficacy beliefs determine people's chosen activities, the extent of their commitment to the goals they choose to pursue, their persistence and their emotional reactions in the face of difficulties. It's also believed that individuals with a high sense of self-efficacy are more successful.

Because of the variety of topics that can be covered in a CAL session, the method can be used to develop a wide range of skills. What's the one thing that all the topics brought to a session have in common? Our research points to self-efficacy.[3] Why?

According to Bandura, one of the most effective ways of creating a strong sense of efficacy is through mastery experiences. Basically, the more successful a person is or the better they perform, the more robust their belief in their personal efficacy. Observation also plays a key role. Seeing one's peers succeed in a difficult situation raises observers' beliefs that they too can master comparable activities. While less influential than observation, verbal persuasion, which can take the form of warnings, questions, advice, and encouragement, can also increase belief in one's capabilities, especially when this persuasion comes from trusted contacts.

Bandura's theory sheds light on how CAL is structured: the first four steps are the observation phase (reframing in Step 3 and sharing experiences in Step 4) and the verbal persuasion phase (asking questions in Step 2, possible solutions and encouragement in Step 4). These steps help boost the participants' confidence and motivate them to act.

This means that Step 5 is the first move towards taking action and the main factor affecting self-efficacy. Once back in their daily lives, each small success, each mastery experience stemming from their action plan, reinforces the participants' belief in their personal efficacy, which generally leads to better performance.

However, again according to Bandura, self-efficacy is not a single perception, but rather a combination of beliefs about the self, each connected to a different area of activity. This means the same person may perceive their self-efficacy differently when it comes to work, sports, or leisure activities. When measuring self-efficacy, ideally, there should be a separate evaluation for each area of interest.[4]

Because CAL focuses primarily on job-related skills, we wanted to know more about its effect on work self-efficacy.[5] See Part 4 for more details about CAL's impact on self-efficacy. To learn more about this concept, see the References section.

Learning journal

In a few words, what is your key insight from this chapter (Step 5)?

How will you help the client prioritize a course of action when many possible ones have been suggested?

How can the participants support each other in implementing their action plan and transferring the new acquired knowledge?

References

1. Bandura, A. (1986). *Social foundations of thought and action: A social cognitive theory*. Prentice-Hall.
2. Bandura, A. (1997). *Self-efficacy: The exercise of control*. W.H. Freeman.

3. Paquet, M., Lafranchise, N., & Sabourin, N. (2021). Des contributions d'une recherche-action pour le codéveloppement. In C. Champagne (Ed.), *Le groupe de codéveloppement. La puissance de l'intelligence collective* (pp. 228–234). Presses de l'Université du Québec.

4. Bandura, A. (2006). Guide for constructing self-efficacy scales. In F. Pajares & T. Urdan (Eds.), *Self-efficacy beliefs of adolescents* (pp. 307–337). Information Age Publishing.

5. Raelin, J. A. (2010). *The work self-efficacy inventory. Sampler set; manual; instrument; scoring guide*. Mind Garden.

Step 6

Takeaways and applications

10

Another key aspect of Codevelopment Action Learning (CAL) is that it must provide all participants with concrete lessons and benefits. Let's see what Emilio and his colleagues take away from Step 6 (Figure 10.1).

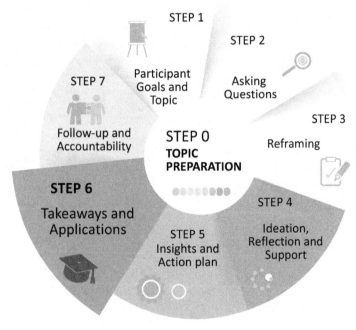

Figure 10.1 CAL's Step 6.

DOI: 10.4324/9781032625720-13

Step 6: takeaways and applications

(Barb) *All that's left for us to do in this session is go through Step 6. That's where we think about what we learned and record our takeaways. It's also the time where we look back at our goals and/ or learning intentions. How did this session helped you reach them?*

I'd also like to hear about the so-called 3 As. First, what did you learn today, what are your Acquired learnings and Takeaways? What Actions are you planning to take? And, what's your Assessment of today's session?

Emilio, you already told us about your action plan in Step 5, but we want to hear from you on the other points, after the consultants have had their turn. I'll give my takeaways as well, but I'll go last.

First, let's take two minutes to note a few points to share.

Who wants to start?

(Gen) *Me. My big takeaway was that I realized the importance of clearly stating our expectations. And, when it comes to onboarding new team members, sending a few emails and holding a few meetings just isn't enough. And I think it's also really important to learn about the managers' own expectations and not just focus on performance targets.*

What about my actions? Well, the end of the quarter is a good time to begin some individual supervision. I'm going to tweak my tracking tool to add questions about my managers' expectations. I'll work on that in the coming weeks.

As for my assessment ... CAL is a really different kind of meeting. The structure means we don't have the same kind of discussions we normally do. It forces us to take the time to really listen, and I like that. Yes, the sessions take time, but if we work more efficiently after- wards, isn't it worth it?

(Barb) *Thanks, Gen. I see you applied your solution to Emilio's problem to your own situation. We'll get back to you later to see how the one-on-one supervision works out.*

In Step 1, you said your goal was to practice your listening skills. I see that in Step 3, you were the first to speak, and here again in Step 6. How do you think you're doing in terms of your goal?

(Gen) *Hmm... I see your point. The session helped me hold back in Steps 4 and 5 and not fall into my old habits, but I see I still have work to do.*

(Barb) *I understand. We can help you with that, if you want. Who's next?*

The participants take turns speaking, ending with Barb and Emilio.

(Barb) *Thanks to everyone for sharing, and thanks again to Emilio for being our brave first client. What a great first session!*

My assessment is that I really enjoyed getting to know you all. I think we're going to have a lot of fun together and I'm sure I'll learn a lot from the experiences you share. My takeaway from today's session is that, despite our best intentions, it's not always easy to accept diversity. We need to find out where our reactions come from.

Max, if you don't mind, I'd like to revisit your idea of diversity and inclusion coaching. That's something I'd like to develop in my own practice in the coming years.

What about you, Emilio?

(Emilio) *I wasn't expecting to enjoy the session as much as I did. To be honest, I was a bit nervous about speaking openly, as I realized that I was reacting emotionally when the new managers got under my skin, even though I couldn't put my finger on it. I think it's great that we can talk about our issues at our own pace and bring up whatever we want.*

For now, I think my biggest takeaway is that I have a habit of focusing almost exclusively on the task at hand and not enough on the person or people doing the work. I noticed that habit back when I was doing my MBA but time passed, my team and I were getting along fine, and I sort of forgot about it. Now, I realize this habit can become a problem when it's time to rally the troops or have difficult conversations. I told you about my actions in Step 5, but I'd like to add that I look forward to getting some coaching to help me better manage my triggers.

(Barb) *Before you go, I'd like to remind you that we'll be doing Step 7 at our next session. First, we'll check in with Emilio and then I'll ask the rest of you how this session helped you tackle some of your daily challenges.*

The only thing left for us to do is confirm who the next client will be. From our initial planning, Nat is next. Does this still work for you?

Step 6 – objectives

The main objective of Step 6 is to ascertain what each participant has learned from the session and define their takeaways. Everyone in the group, including the client and facilitator, are asked to share their thoughts on three topics. To help people remember them, we called them the 3 As.

First, the group discusses their Acquired Learnings & Takeaways: what they learned, thought about, and realized. Next, everyone is given the opportunity to share the Actions they're planning to take, based on the discussions in the first five steps. Finally, participants give their Assessment, saying how they feel about the session.

Step 6 is also a good time to look back at the learning goals and/or intentions from Step 1. How have I changed, and how has my original learning intention evolved?

While the client is the person who comes away from each session with the most actionable plan, the consultants and facilitator are encouraged to think about how they will transfer what they've learned to their own work. For example, how can active listening, asking questions, and giving supportive feedback practiced in CAL be transferred to other situations?

Step 6 – benefits

Learn from each other and acquire the habit of thinking about their own work

Step 6 is a part of the CAL method that enables participants to focus on learning not just when they act but also about their actions.

This is where we can see session's impact on the participants and the group. Did they learn anything? Did they get any closer to achieving their goals and/or learning intentions? Did they improve their listening, questioning, or other skills? Have they mastered the CAL method?

This step teaches participants to take the time to step back, a process that's often forgotten in today's fast-paced world. However, these moments are critical to developing the reflective mindset that people need if they want to learn how to manage their most important work resource: themself![1]

The reflex to step back learned in this step can be transferred into the participants' daily lives, as CAL helps participants take the first step towards a reflective mindset. After this session, participants often say, "We realized that reflecting on our experiences helps us learn from our mistakes and find new ways of seeing situations."

Facilitating Step 6

While facilitating Step 6 may seem to be a relatively straightforward process, this step is a crucial phase in taking what participants learn to the next level, i.e., in moving beyond simple problem solving. The CAL method's core belief is the importance of integrating the reflective mindset with the action mindset.

First, each consultant shares their 3 As, and if they feel they achieved their goal and/or learning intention.

Because participants tend not to practice this kind of intentional reflective mindset much in their day-to-day lives, we notice that they have to work at reflecting on what they learned and experienced during a CAL session.

The facilitator can give the consultants some suggestions to help their feedback be more specific:

Acquired learnings and takeaways

–   What I learned about the topic
–   What I learned about myself or my abilities
–   What I learned about the group

Actions

–   Actions I will integrate into my daily routine
–   New methods I will try at work
–   Things I will do differently

Assessment

- My favourite part. What I especially liked and/or was surprised by
- What inspired me
- What I would like the group to do differently
- This is a good time for the facilitator to ask the participants questions, to draw out anyone who hasn't yet shared their progress on achieving their learning intention and/or goal they shared in Step 1.

Next, it's the facilitators turn to say what they have learned. The client has the final word, speaking about any of the 3 As that they haven't already shared in Step 5.

To make it easier for the facilitator to keep track of the participants' progress towards achieving their goals, we suggest they write down the actions the participants intend to take. This makes it easier to ask them about this during Step 7. This enables the facilitator to remind the participants of their met and unmet goals at subsequent or in between sessions.

Finally, if needed, the facilitator can suggest relevant follow-up materials to the participants between sessions, such as articles, videos, and other educational resources.

Facilitation tips – Managing time

Enhancing learning by reflecting on our actions is a core part of the CAL method and the key to its success. When Step 6 is rushed, CAL is reduced to a mere problem-solving group, with fewer and less beneficial learning opportunities.

The group must be sure to manage the time it spends on Steps 1–5, to ensure there is enough time left for Step 6.

Step 6 – Takeaways and actions

Main objectives

Discuss the group's 3 As: share their Acquired Learnings & Takeaways, their Actions and give their Assessment.

Client's and consultants' roles

Discuss what they've learned (Acquired Learnings and Takeaways) and the ideas they will put into action (Actions).

Share their Assessment of the session: the extent to which they achieved their learning goals and their overall satisfaction.

(Continued)

Step 6 – Takeaways and actions

Facilitator's role

The same as other participants.

If this has not already been done, choose the client for the next session and set a moment for Step 0.

Record the group's takeaways and actions.

Suggested time: ≈20 min

Tool: CAL think sheet – Seven steps (see Appendix)

Table 10.1 Summary table for Step 6

Adult learning and reflective practice

In the 1960s, Malcolm S. Knowles advanced the idea of "andragogy,"[2] a learning theory for adults as distinct from the pedagogy governing children.

The theory of andragogy posits that adults learn best when they are able to experience, problem-solve, and reflect on their actions and when they are able to develop their own learning intentions, especially when these intentions are directly related to their work and/or personal life.

As part of the goal-setting process done in Step 1, Step 6 provides an opportunity to connect participants' goals to their lived experience by focusing on the progress they have made.

This step also gives participants the time they need to start using the kind of reflective practice outlined in the adult learning theory. What are my takeaways from the CAL session? How can I apply them to my own situation or experiences? What specific actions can I take to improve my own work?

Based on the principles of reflective practice defined by Donald Schön,[3] the author suggests that learning how to be reflective can start with "reflection on action," or reflecting after the event, to review, analyse, and evaluate the situation and come up with new ways of thinking and acting. As Jonathan Gosling and Henry Mintzberg so aptly said, "You must appreciate the past if you wish to use the present to get to a better future."[1]

While reflecting on an action after the fact is important, through CAL, participants can also acquire the habit of reflecting on their behaviour as it happens, a process Schön calls "reflection in action." The goal of acquiring this skill is learning how to think about our effectiveness in the moment, as well as evaluating a given situation's learning potential. Acquiring this skill gives participants more control over situations and hence over their performance.

Learning journal

In a few words, what is your key insight from this chapter (Step 6)?

How is a CAL group different from a problem-solving group?

How important is stepping back and reflective practice in your organization? Why is this?

References

1. Gosling, J., & Mintzberg, H. (2003). The five minds of a manager. *Harvard Business Review*, March/April. https://hbr.org/2003/11/the-five-minds-of-a-manager
2. Knowles, M. S., Holton, E. F., & Swanson, R. A. (2015). *The adult learner: The definitive classic in adult education and human resource development* (8th ed.). Routledge.
3. Schön, D. A. (2017). *The reflective practitioner: How professionals think in action*. Routledge.

Step 7

11

Follow-up and accountability

The final and most important part of the Codevelopment Action Learning (CAL) method is taking action and moving forward. Let's see how far Emilio has come since the last session (Figure 11.1).

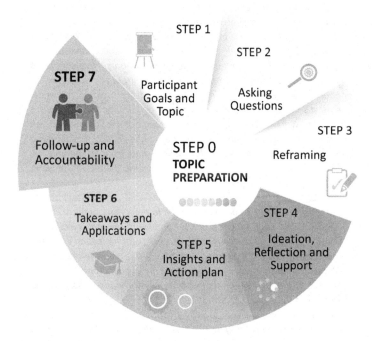

Figure 11.1 CAL's Step 7.

DOI: 10.4324/9781032625720-14

Step 7: follow-up and accountability

Nat is the client for Steps 0–6 of the second CAL session. In Step 7, the group goes over the progress Emilio – the previous session's client – has made and Barb asks the rest of the group what impact CAL has had on their work.

(Barb) *A big thank you to Nat for volunteering to be our client today. I'm already looking forward to hearing how your team meeting went at the next session.*

At the end of the last session, we said that Emilio would give us an update on his topic and on how things are going with his team. He and I exchanged a few emails to help him prepare his remarks. Emilio, can you remind us what your goal was and tell us what you've been up to since the last session?

(Emilio) *My goal was to become a better leader for my new team. I also wanted to find out why I sometime felt uncomfortable interacting with them, so I could either do something about it or delegate if ever I found myself getting overwhelmed.*

So, I started by asking my VP if I could use part of my budget for coaching. She immediately said yes. My coach and I have already met twice, and we've had time to establish my goals. He also shared some resources to help me plan my team's strategic retreat, which happened last week. We did a bunch of team-building activities; I think it's already helped me understand them better. We had a meeting to work on the communication plan but it's not finished yet; we ran out of time. But the reactions were positive, and that's a good sign. In fact, they were so enthusiastic, I had trouble chairing the meeting! Anyway, we have two further meetings planned to finish it. I'm really happy with the way things are going.

(Barb) *That's great news, Emilio. Now, what do you have left to do, and what resources can you access to help you get there?*

(Emilio) *As I said, I have a clearer picture of my managers' motivations, and that's certainly helpful, but my communication style still sometimes rubs them the wrong way. That's one of my two coaching goals: to change the way I communicate my expectations.*

(Barb) *Out of everything that was shared at the last session, what did you find the most relevant or helpful?*

(Emilio) *The question as to why I still didn't know them and the suggestion to do something together as a group. When I thought about it, I realized I was in a vicious circle. When I'm angry, I'm less likely to be interested in getting to know my managers. And, when I take less of an interest in them, there's no way to change the situation so I feel stuck – and angry! I know I've been doing really good work these past few years but now, with the new team, I don't think I can manage alone. To be honest, it was tough to admit that. But, in the end, nobody forced me to get a coach. And, it doesn't actually hurt – too much! (Laughs)*

(Barb) *What about the others? Gen, you said wanted to start doing some individual supervision with your managers. How did that go?*

(Gen) *It went really well, thanks. The meetings are almost finished.*
(Barb) *Can you tell us a bit more? And, were the group discussions helpful?*

Barb continues, asking the previous clients about implementing their action plan, and asking the consultants how they could apply what they learned in Step 6 to their own situation. What insights were they able to translate into action, and how did the group discussion help them? She concludes by answering these questions herself.

Step 7 – objectives

Every CAL session ends with a look back at the previous session. So, in Step 7, the previous client tells the group about the progress they made towards their learning goal and whatever actions they still need to take. They also share how they feel about their progress. This is also a good time to name and reinforce any lessons that have been learned at the individual and group level.

Basically, the main objective of Step 7 is to encourage participants to put into action the knowledge they have acquired, as this increases the likelihood they will apply some of it to their work.

As previously mentioned, CAL is more than just a problem-solving or discussion group. In order to achieve real results, each participant must adopt a learner mindset (previously discussed in Step 1). Doing so enables them to focus on and be open to the various courses of action that emerge through the questioning and sharing activities. It's then up to the participants to adapt these courses of action to their situation and to be bold, to dare, to take action!

Step 7 – benefits

Step 7 is where participants grasp the true impact of everything that's happened so far: the capacities they've acquired, the actions they've taken, and the progress they've made.

Because of this, Step 7 also enables the group to show the organization that's supporting the CAL process the concrete gains that have been made and how these can be applied in real-life work situations. Although what happens in CAL stays in CAL, the organization still needs proof that the sessions are effective, in order to continue supporting them.

At this point, the group can decide what will be reported to the organization, and how often, i.e., halfway through and at the end, for instance.

If everyone agrees, the group can use the facilitator's notes as the basis for a report that includes the following de-identified information:

- A general description of the topics they've discussed
- From those discussions, the knowledge they've acquired
- Using that knowledge, the actions they've taken
- Based on those actions, the progress they've made

Facilitating Step 7

First, the facilitator asks the client about their plan of action: did they achieve their goal? What action did they take? How did that work out? What steps in the right direction did they take? If the client experienced setbacks or had doubts about their chosen course of action, these should also be shared, as learning sometimes means making mistakes or not taking the right path. In that case, the group can offer its support.

Next, the facilitator asks the client if there are any items in their action plan they still have to work on and if they want to return to these items with the group at a later date. The final question is about how CAL has helped the client in their work. Hearing about the group's concrete benefits helps motivate and encourage the participants.

To stimulate discussion and highlight CAL's impact, the facilitator can ask the client other questions, such as:

- What best practices could be shared with a co-worker who couldn't join our group?
- What would I have overlooked if I hadn't participated in this session?
- What's the biggest "Aha!" moment I took away from a/the CAL session(s)?
- What am I doing differently now because of what I learned in a/ the CAL session(s)?
- What skills have I developed so far? Active listening? Effective questioning? Other skills?
- What collective value have we created? What have we learned from each other that we would like to share outside of the group?

Finally, the facilitator quickly runs through the same questions with the consultants. They usually have less to share than the client, but they too may have put some ideas into action between sessions.

These questions and the attendant discussion are a way to define the participants' learning and progress, with the goal of stimulating their development beyond the CAL group.

The answers to the aforementioned questions can serve as the basis for deciding what will be shared, in de-identified form, with the organization, or shared outside the group so that other people in the organization can be inspired by the group's progress.

Facilitation tips – managing time

To increase the effectiveness of Step 7, the facilitator can make sure the following session's client has the Step 7 preparation worksheet (see Appendix). This helps the client be prepared for the questions they will be asked during the session.

Time permitting, the clients from previous sessions can tell the group about any further progress they've made.

If the previous session's client isn't ready to talk about their progress, you can come back to their situation later. Some action plans take longer to implement than others. If that's the case with this particular client, it's better to just check in with them briefly during this step and then move on to another client, rather than forcing them to give an extensive update too soon.

Step 7 – Follow-up and accountability

Main objectives

Follow up on how the client implemented their action plan, on the group's individual and collective learning, and on the actions taken.

Since Step 7 involves revisiting situations previously addressed by the group, the first workshop obviously does not include this step. Also, Step 7 can be placed at the beginning or the end of a session, depending on the group's preference.

Client's role

The client (or clients) from the previous session(s) talks about the achievements and challenges they faced implementing their action plan and identifies the insights and lessons learned.

The client also says what they still have to work on.

Consultants' role

Reflect on how these insights and lessons could be applied to their own situation and work.

If applicable, share any of their own actions that were influenced by the CAL group.

Facilitator's role

Before the session, send the Step 7 preparation worksheet to the client.

Ask the client (or clients) from the previous session(s) to talk about what they've done since the workshop ended.

Ask the consultants to share how they've been applying what they learned.

Start a discussion on what the group has learned, and what lessons could be shared outside the group, i.e., within the organization, for instance.

Share relevant resources to complement the lessons learned: articles, books, videos, etc.

Draw up a list of best practices mentioned during the session and send it to the participants.

Suggested time: ≈ 15 min

Tool : Step 7 preparation worksheet; CAL Think sheet – Seven steps (see Appendix)

Table 11.1 Summary table for Step 7

Experiential learning

Step 7 is designed to ensure that CAL group participants go through an entire learning cycle, as defined by David Kolb in his theory of experiential learning.[1] By going through the entire cycle, participants are more likely to acquire both thorough and lasting learning and are more likely to transfer it to their work.

The first stage of the experiential learning cycle is Concrete Experience, which the learner (in CAL, the client) presents in Step 1. Steps 2–4 correspond the cycle's Reflective Observations stages. Through questioning, feedback, and shared experiences, participants explore the client's experience.

Steps 5 and 6 are where the group establishes the possible actions that can be taken. It's also where the session's lessons and insights are integrated into the action models that participants previously used (discussed in Step 4). This corresponds to the cycle's Abstract Conceptualization stage.

If the group was content to be simply a discussion group, the cycle – and hence the learning – wouldn't be complete! The real actions the participants are prepared to take, which correspond to the cycle's Active Experimentation stage, have not yet been identified.

This is where Step 7 comes in, which adds a level of accountability by making participants responsible for actively pursuing the ideas that emerge from CAL. Participants can't use the CAL group as a place to simply think about their issue. They know that they will be asked about their progress between sessions. At this point, when they present another concrete experience to the group for discussion, they have essentially completed the process. Although action is the basis for learning, lasting learning cannot take place without reflecting back on that action.

Participants can take their support even further by deciding together what learning style they want to follow. Again, as discussed in Kolb's theory, there are nine different styles.[2]

For example, "the initiating style is characterized by the ability to initiate action in order to deal with experiences and situations. It involves active experimentation and concrete experience" (p. 14). The "deciding style is characterized by the ability to use theories and models to decide on problem solutions and courses of action. It combines abstract conceptualization and active experimentation" (p. 15).

Having a better understanding of each person's learning style could enable the CAL group to make better decisions in terms of the questions asked (Step 2) and the possible solutions suggested (Step 4). Returning to the two styles mentioned above, initiating style people learn best by trying different approaches, while deciding style people must have a theory that provides the basis for their actions.

If you want to know more about experiential learning, see the books listed in the References section. If you'd like to know more about learning styles, the book *How you learn is how you live: Using nine ways of learning to transform your life*,[3] by Kay Peterson and David Kolb is sure to interest you.

Learning journal

In a few words, what is your key insight from this chapter (Step 7)?

What resources would you use to support CAL participants' accountability for developing and successfully implementing their action plans?

After reading the last few chapters, how has your understanding of learning changed? If so, how?

References

1. Kolb, A. A., & Kolb, D. A. (2013). *The Kolb learning style inventory 4.0. A comprehensive guide to the theory, psychometrics, research on validity and educational applications*. Experience Based Learning Systems.
2. Kolb, D. A. (2015). *Experiential learning: Experience as the source of learning and development* (2nd ed.). Pearson Education, Inc.
3. Peterson, K., & Kolb, D. A. (2017). *How you learn is how you live: Using nine ways of learning to transform your life*. Berrett-Koehler Publishers, Inc.

Is your organization ready for Codevelopment Action Learning?

Part 3

Ten winning conditions

12

Now that you've read Parts 1 and 2, what's going through your mind?

— *I've got a better idea of what* Codevelopment Action Learning's (CAL) *all about now, and I can see how it could work really well to move projects forward in my workplace.*
— *I'd love to get my team involved in a CAL group, but I don't know how to ask them or what to do to get it started.*
— *I can see CAL working with that group. I'm excited to get the pilot up and running!*
— *How do I become a CAL facilitator?*

Or....

— *Sounds interesting, but I'm just not sure it'll work with my team.*
— *It sounds great, but how do I get it off the ground?*
— *I don't know ... To me, it seems like a case of the blind leading the blind.*
— *Maybe CAL is just another fad or the latest buzz word?*

Try it; embrace it!

Based on our experience facilitating, teaching, and researching the method, the best way to get people to understand the CAL approach is to have them try it. That's why our motto is "Try it; embrace it." However, that statement comes with a major caveat: to achieve lasting results, CAL groups must be set up and run according to certain conditions.

This chapter describes the ten winning conditions needed for CAL groups to be effective.

For a detailed description of two successful rollouts, see Chapter 14, which describes how CAL was implemented over six years in the city of Laval (Canada), and Chapter 15, which describes a similar scenario over nine years at the Quebec Order of Chartered Human Resource and Industrial Relations Counsellors.

DOI: 10.4324/9781032625720-16

As mentioned in Part 1, Chapter 2, the CAL approach can be implemented in two ways: either internally within an organization, i.e., with leaders or professionals from different departments or functions, or with project managers working on different initiatives. It can also be implemented with participants from different organizations or specialties, such as CEOs or HR leaders from different companies; directors of different schools, entrepreneurs, etc.

Now, let's take a closer look at the various winning conditions by considering some concrete examples (see Figure 12.1).

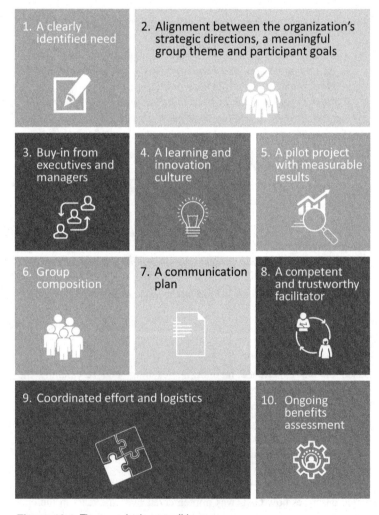

Figure 12.1 The ten winning conditions.

1. A clearly identified need

As mentioned in Part 1, Chapter 1, CAL can address issues related to col-laboration, performance and transformation, and development. In other words, it can help people co-create solutions, accelerate their goals, and grow through mutual learning.

One commonly observed mistake when organizations were launching CAL groups was to implement them without having first identified a clear need.

When implementing any training or development program or any organizational development initiative, a comprehensive needs analysis should be done first, before deciding to set up CAL groups. The analysis should explore the various factors that need to be taken into account: organizational factors (context, strategic alignment, learning climate); task-related factors (what abilities the person should develop in order to perform better in their role and tasks); and individual factors (target audience, motivation, receptiveness to the approach).

The analysis can collect data in several ways, through surveys, interviews with key stakeholders, focus groups and by reviewing admin-istrative data, for instance.

A healthcare setting example

The HR department at a Montreal hospital wanted to support their managers' ongoing development (organizational factor). The results of a 360-degree feedback assessment indicated a need to develop their influencing and change management skills (task-related factor). When the HR department suggested to managers that they use CAL to develop these skills, the managers agreed and were motivated to start (individual factor).

Facilitation tips – quick needs analysis

Some CAL facilitators were so eager to implement the approach that they set up a group (or groups) without ensuring the goals were aligned with an actual organizational need. Needless to say, these CAL groups were short-lived and had little or no impact.

For better results, the facilitators should at least have performed a quick needs analysis by talking to executives and key stakeholders,[1] to align their groups with an objective that was both clearly identified and had the support of upper management.

2. Alignment between the organization's strategic directions, a meaningful group theme, and participant goals

A CAL group's success depends on its ability to create meaning for the participants. This meaning can be created in a number of ways.

First, the group must decide on a **unifying theme** that will bring it together and help participants understand the group's purpose. The theme is jointly developed by the decision makers behind CAL and/or group members and should take into account issues and/or concerns that are shared by the organization and group members.

A purposeful CAL group theme guides participants in choosing topics that are aligned with the organization's strategic direction. The theme should be specific enough to focus the group's work, yet still allow participants the freedom to propose topics that are meaningful to them. As previously discussed, leaders can meet to develop their influencing and change management skills. In Part 2, we also followed a group of managers who met to successfully carry out a transformation project. The examples in this chapter provide several other theme ideas.

We also suggest participants establish **development goals** for themselves when the group begins. They can then use these goals to help choose which topic to select, as well as the learning goals/intentions that participants set for themselves in Step 1 of the sessions (see Part 2, Chapter 5).

In intra-organizational CAL, these development goals can be part of the participants' competency development plan and discussed with their manager, thereby increasing the manager's buy-in and support of the CAL participant. For example, a leader who wants to develop their influence might bring up a topic that involves employees who refuse to work together.

Ideally, HR should recognize CAL as an official training activity. As previously mentioned, this means that training content should be tied to the organization's strategic directions. The hours invested in CAL should therefore count as time spent on training and development and be recorded as such in the participants' employee file.

CAL deployment in the largest financial cooperative in North America

The cooperative provided training to the board members of its internal Young Managers Network to become CAL facilitators. The young leaders also received coaching when the approach was implemented in a network of 300 young leaders.

The organization's purpose in launching this initiative was to provide support to the Young Intern Director Program so it could implement CAL groups that would enable young leaders to grow and develop a "Human Collaborative Leadership mindset" (the group's theme) and promote cross-functional collaboration.

The managers responsible for CAL were convinced that the groups could help develop a high-performing collaborative culture aligned with the organization's cooperative mission (the strategic direction).

This strategic alignment gained traction when three top executives took on the client role in a number of fishbowl-style CAL demos at the annual Young Managers Network Conference. The executive-clients took advantage of the discussions to gain insight into ways of accelerating the cooperative's priority projects, in accordance with its strategic plan. The sessions generated a huge number of creative ideas, which was highly motivating for the young leaders, and encouraged them to implement the ideas in their own units (participant goals).

This ground-breaking initiative showed the executive team's commitment to CAL as an effective way for young leaders to co-create solutions, accelerate their projects and grow. Afterwards, many CAL groups were deployed and the CAL method gained reputation as one of the key action learning approaches to be used in leadership development programs.[2]

3. Buy-in from executives and managers

As with any organizational change or development initiative, those CAL initiatives that lasted longer than one year had the support of executives and CAL participants' managers. This support could be expressed in a variety of ways, such as: providing the required resources for group rollouts (including paid participation); becoming CAL ambassadors and sponsoring the project; taking part in CAL-related promotional activities; and encouraging leaders and employees to participate in groups.

One all-too-common mistake managers make when launching CAL groups is forgetting to ensure that participation is completely voluntary and that participants have the time, resources and support to commit to the group for the entire process.

For example, some managers might routinely ask their employees to skip attending the CAL group and do other work instead. This not only impacts the groups' effectiveness, but also wastes resources (i.e., the facilitator's salary and other participants' time) that could have been better allocated elsewhere.

If the executives and managers involved don't already support the approach, they can be brought on board in several ways. They can be introduced to CAL through a demonstration or pilot group (winning condition #5), during which they can see the benefits (see Part 4). They can also be involved at various stages of the communication plan (winning condition #7). Another option is for each participant to discuss the matter with their manager, to ensure the latter is familiar with the participant's learning intentions/goals and is therefore able to formally commit to supporting them in the process. (See Appendix for the CAL participation form.) However, the most obvious way is simply to tell them about the positive outcomes of CAL groups (winning conditions #5 and #10). See Chapter 13 for more examples of executive and manager involvement, as illustrated by the city of Laval case.

An IT company example

A company specializing in radiology technology gave team leaders who had just completed their leadership development training the opportunity to participate in CAL groups. Participation in this second development opportunity was voluntary. Because the participants' managers knew the benefits of CAL, having applied the lessons leaned there to their own work, they encouraged their team leaders to join the group. Despite the pressure to succeed placed on the group, participation rates were surprisingly high.

The then-HR VP noted that CAL built bridges between different parts of the company and increased feelings of trust between colleagues. Trust is an essential ingredient for collaboration, and a crucial part of every company's performance.

Facilitation tips – foster engagement in CAL groups

We encourage each participant to complete and sign the CAL participation form (see Appendix). This tool allows participants to describe their learning intentions/goals and commit to the CAL principles. In certain cases, the participant's manager can also be encouraged to sign the form as well, in a joint commitment to the CAL journey. After completion, this form is sent to the CAL facilitator who reviews the content that can be used to support upcoming Step 0 Topic preparation discussions.

4. A learning and innovation culture

One of the key winning conditions for ensuring long-term implementation of CAL groups is the existence of a learning and innovative culture. To find out if this your organization fulfils this condition, consider the following questions.[3,4]

Does the organization's mission promote its own constant improvement and growth? Does it value its employees' continuous learning and personal development? What mechanisms has the organization implemented to support shared learning and knowledge transfer?

And if learning and growth are indeed valued, how do managers and employees currently pursue those goals? Are there alternatives to traditional training? Would managers and employees enjoy learning from each other, or is their environment too competitive?

If you're not sure what kind of culture your organization has, we suggest you assess it when doing your needs analysis, using one of the many questionnaires created for that purpose. See the work of Cameron & Quinn and Marsick & Watkins in the References section.[5,6]

For starters, we recommend identifying prominent leaders who want to do things differently. They are the ones that are prepared to bring about change in the organization and ready to start implementing CAL with their teams.

A large healthcare organization example

A large healthcare organization near Montreal, Canada launched a CAL pilot initiative that consisted of five groups. The groups' success spread throughout the large healthcare organization by word of mouth.

Two years later, more than 15 CAL groups in various departments were up and running. Their goal was to support managers and employees in their ongoing efforts to keep up with evolving best practices, as a way of coping with ever-changing demands.

Based on its success, senior managers decided to make CAL groups part of their strategic development initiatives.

The HR Director took the necessary steps to add CAL to the list of official training activities, a measure that had the combined benefit of increasing participation and supporting the development of the organization's learning culture.

---

5. A pilot project with measurable results

To help you set up a CAL group (or groups), we recommend starting off with a pilot project. The pilot should include a mid- and end-of-cycle evaluation to measure the group's impact, thereby enabling decision makers to determine if CAL is a good fit for the organization. As previously mentioned, the hard data generated by the evaluations also help ensure buy-in from executives and the participants' managers by providing them with a foretaste of CAL's benefits.

The evaluation must be set up well in advance and include specific metrics. For more details on what it should entail, see winning condition

#10. Part 4 also includes several examples of metrics that can be used to measure CAL's various benefits.

If it's not possible to set up a pilot project, we recommend holding a CAL "discovery session" in which key stakeholders (decision makers and/or leaders) can experience the approach and its benefits first-hand. However, the CAL coordinators (see winning condition #9) must work out every detail of this session in advance to ensure its a success: secure an experienced facilitator, choose the topic carefully, and select the client.

Part 4 includes several examples of metrics that can be used to measure CAL's various benefits.

A municipal example

A Canadian municipality decided to establish a project management culture to promote innovation and efficiency. To help employees develop their project management skills, the municipality set up a CAL pilot group. Three-hour sessions with volunteer participants and facilitated by an external facilitator were scheduled every five weeks for 12 months. The pilot was a resounding success and the groups ran for several years. Next, the HR manager received training to lead the groups. A video with participant success stories was created and was such a hit, it became part of the training for other internal CAL facilitators.[7] Then, the Administration Head of the municipality was invited to facilitate an important fishbowl-style CAL demo in a large-scale forum with other municipalities across Quebec.

---

6. Group composition

When setting up a group, we recommend prioritizing the factors listed in Chapter 2, as they describe the ideal CAL composition. However, if you're turning existing groups or teams into a CAL group, we urge you to be on the lookout for the following characteristics as, based on our first-hand experience and research, they will significantly impact the method's success.

Factors affecting a group's effectiveness:

- Groups are too large or too small (fewer than five or more than ten participants).
- Participants are volunteered by their managers rather than signing up voluntarily, or are not open to group/peer learning.
- There is unresolved or poorly managed conflict between participants.

- The group is unwilling or unable to think outside the box or be open to new ideas.
- The group's hierarchical culture discourages open discussion.
- Even if the group's structure is flat, some participants consider themselves experts, are resistant to peer-based, experiential and reflective learning, and so tend to dominate the conversation.

Another healthcare organization example

To recruit volunteers for a large, organized program after some initial pilot groups, a large regional healthcare organization followed our recommendations and did the following:

- A director took on the client role in a large, fishbowl-style CAL discovery session. He was an excellent client: open to the new experience and willing to set aside his own opinions and learn from others. During the demo, the facilitator explained the criteria that should be used when creating groups: they should include leaders from different departments, a mix of new and experienced leaders, and so on.
- Interested leaders were introduced to CAL at an off-site forum.
- The CAL coordinator held an inspiring information session, that included some opening comments from the directors in charge of implementing CAL, a video about the approach, and success stories from past participants.

The first few sessions were open. Participants who felt uncomfortable with the approach were free to drop out.

---

7. A communication plan

Before CAL can be implemented, communications must be sent out in order to: get senior managers on board, obtain resources, recruit participants, and secure managers' support for the process during every phase of the rollout.

As with any communication plan, the first step is to decide on the target audience – in this case, the executives at the organizational level, the participants' managers at the team/group level and the participants themselves.

The CAL project coordinator responsible for the communication plan should ask themself: What's the strategic direction behind the initiative? What are the group's objectives and themes? Can the benefits of CAL (see Part 4) be shared to encourage participation? Sending out the condensed results of the organization's past groups is a good way to raise awareness of CAL and get buy-in from stakeholders.

These messages can be communicated in a variety of ways, most of which will require some resources. For instance, the CAL coordinator could write a short text introducing the CAL groups that includes: a definition, the goals, the prerequisites for participating, the expected benefits, and so on. The person could also create one or more videos with ambassador endorsements from executives or former participants, resources for facilitators, pages on the organization's intranet or social network, internal media articles, etc.

We recommend that organizations give their CAL project a name, to promote buy-in.

An university example

During the first year of the CAL rollout, the Rector of Université du Québec à Montréal (UQAM) and the HR Director at the Vice-Rector's Office for Administration and Finance acted as ambassadors for the approach. In subsequent years, group participants became ambassadors for the approach by being actively involved in promoting and recruiting their peers. See Part 4, Chapter 17 for the full story of UQAM's rollout.

---

8. A competent and trustworthy facilitator

It's crucial to find a facilitator who understands the CAL approach and who will guide and support the group throughout the process. More importantly, the participants must feel they can trust the facilitator. Another key question is: should the group be facilitated by an external facilitator or an internal resource? The following chapter provides more details on how to become a CAL facilitator, as well as the key skills you must have or develop to fill the role.

CAL to accelerate the integration of young woman immigrants

Written with the contribution of Régine Alende Tshombokongo, Founder and General Manager, CEJFI ("Centre d'encadrement des jeunes femmes immigrantes")

The CEJFI – a dynamic social sector organization based in Montreal, Canada – has decided to integrate CAL into their practices to support the mission of accelerating the integration of young immigrant women.

The General Manager had a vision to deploy CAL at three levels: (1) within her management committee to improve collaboration and teamwork; (2) in a development and integration journey over a period of three years, to allow young women to help each other, find solutions together while improving their communication and collaboration skills; (3) to equip members of her team to accompany groups in a different way.

Two experienced external facilitators supported the CEJFI in these initiatives. Firstly, the entire team was able to live and experience CAL sessions. Members quickly volunteered to be internal facilitators and implement CAL sessions during monthly team meetings. Then, regular coaching sessions by one of the external facilitators was offered for further development of facilitation capabilities.

CAL was a great success with the participants, as evidenced by survey results:

- CAL fostered the establishment of mutual aid and trust between us: 4.95/5
- I recommend CAL to my colleagues: 4.90/5

To date, CAL continues to be driven internally within the CEJFI team. In addition, the approach is deployed in new journeys for women entrepreneurs.

The use of a CAL facilitator profile to select internal facilitators

To help select and recruit a team of internal CAL facilitators, the previously mentioned regional healthcare centre created a chart listing the facilitator's required capabilities. The chart also enabled facilitators to self-assess their abilities and to identify the professional development activities they could sign up for to become better at facilitating CAL groups.

9. Coordinated effort and logistics

Businesses that implement CAL groups must be prepared to provide resources for project coordination and logistics. Especially in large organizations, participants and managers appreciate having a single point of contact, such as a project manager or coordination team, to answer their questions. Some kind of coordination is necessary to create groups that meet the chosen criteria, to set up online sessions or to reserve rooms for in-person sessions.

The person or team tasked with this role must therefore have a broad range of abilities, such as project management and leadership skills, as well as some influence, to promote CAL and create an effective communication plans. Quantitative and qualitative data collection and analysis skills are also essential for conducting evaluations or providing groups and facilitators with the tools for conducting them.

A last healthcare organization example

The same healthcare organization already had 23 active CAL groups. The director tasked a project manager with orchestrating another large-scale rollout. This person acted as a CAL ambassador, implemented the communication plan, recruited internal facilitators and supervised their training. She also organized demo sessions for every department, set up the CAL groups, monitored their progress and ensured they were formally evaluated. Thanks to her work, the facilitators were able to focus on supporting their CAL groups.

---

10. Ongoing benefits assessment

Like other approaches to supporting and developing people, such as mentoring programs and communities of practice, it can be difficult if not impossible to accurately determine CAL's return on investment (ROI).

Given this difficulty, we suggest measuring the return on expectations (ROE)[8] instead, and deciding how to measure this metric before the groups are even launched. One important factor to consider is: who are the CAL stakeholders and what are their expectations?

For example, in addition to participant satisfaction, leaders, managers, and HR professionals will want to know: What have participants learned? Can we notice them using new skills (grow)? Have teams improved their ability to collaborate (co-create) across silos? Are projects and goals being achieved faster (accelerate) to improve overall performance? Did participants implement new solutions to help bring about changes in their organization? Did they feel more confident in their role, taking ownership of activities and increasing their sense of self-efficacy? What was achieved in terms of organizational goals? Did the group achieve the goals related to its theme?

When launching a CAL group, we recommend asking participants for their expectations. What will they be proud to have achieved together? What progress do they expect to make regarding their learning intentions? How will their participation benefit them personally?

For a CAL initiative to be considered an investment and not simply an expense, decision makers, managers and even the participants themselves must clearly see the benefits.

We also know that organizational leadership changes frequently. Another advantage of hard data is that it provides a compelling argument for continuing the CAL groups, thereby making the initial investment more cost-effective.

Despite the popular belief that conducting evaluations is tedious and time-consuming, in this case, the person (or team) responsible simply has to establish, at the outset, the metrics that need to be measured and allocate the resources needed to collect and analyse the data. However, it's crucial to ensure that the person (or team) who carries out the evaluation has the necessary skills to do so.

The groups can be involved in choosing the methods and metrics to be used, and can also be given the tools to collect the data. Halfway through and at the end of the cycle, some short surveys, participants' qualitative assessments and a few interviews are enough to generate the necessary data.

See Part 4, that discusses the outcomes of CAL, for more details on benefits assessment.

Another municipal example

The city of Laval (Canada) had launched CAL groups for managers several years ago; at that time, it had developed a plan to evaluate the groups' impact. The plan involved:

- Having participants identify their learning intentions at the start of the groups.
- Conducting short evaluation surveys and qualitative assessments with participants mid-way through and at the end of the cycle.
- Interviewing participants' managers.
- Organizing regular facilitator meetings to take the pulse of their groups, find out how their facilitator experience is going, and support them.
- Establishing metrics based on data gathered from the aforementioned sources: participation rates, theme alignment, group dynamics, learning outcomes, etc.

See Chapter 14 for the full story of the City of Laval's rollout.

What to do if certain winning conditions are missing?

If your organization doesn't have all the preconditions for launching CAL groups, don't be discouraged. Instead, be the change you want to see! To do so, we suggest identifying the assets in your teams, or the organization as a whole, that could be used to help create the right winning conditions.

For example:

- Could senior management be introduced to CAL through other training and development activities, such as a community of practice or a session held during a leaders' forum?
- Are there any CAL-friendly leaders who would be ready to try out the approach with their teams   or like-minded peers?
- Could you invite an experienced CAL facilitator to present the approach to senior management?
- Could you set up a low-budget pilot project?
- Will your organization soon be undergoing a major transformation in which the CAL approach would be extremely useful?

Remember, the most far-reaching organizational changes often occur through organic and viral means.[9]

Other creative ways to use CAL

As previously mentioned, the group is one of CAL's most basic features.

But what if it's not possible to get people together for regular, scheduled meetings? Can you launch the CAL approach in your organization without this condition? Can you hold a single session and still get results?

The answer is YES!

But, how?

The answer lies in CAL's three fundamental attributes: an effective method, powerful guiding principles and three key roles.

A leadership development forum example in a large high-tech firm

Sixteen 120-min CAL sessions were held simultaneously as part of a leadership development forum for 120 leaders from a large Canadian telecommunications firm. The groups were led by a combination of experienced internal and external facilitators.

CAL was chosen because these leaders preferred to learn through action and experience. A previous CAL pilot project involving six leaders had produced positive results.

Reaction to the 120-min single sessions was overwhelmingly positive. Afterwards, leaders mentioned that it was one of the best forums they had ever attended. The CEO claimed that he had never seen his leadership team so full of positive energy and motivation as they were in that moment.

In addition to the high levels of participant satisfaction, many other positive outcomes were noted. Open, honest discussions about real-life situations fostered an atmosphere of trust and creativity that enabled participants to leave with concrete solutions they could rapidly apply – an outcome the CEO was happy to observe.

Limitations of the CAL approach

As discussed in Part 4, a well-implemented CAL group can produce many positive outcomes. However, as practitioners and researchers, we feel obliged to mention that CAL is not a panacea, nor is it infallible. Learning from experience and action is not always possible, nor is it always the best approach.

In addition to the absence of the previously listed winning conditions, here are a few reasons why CAL *won't* work.

Collective capacity

According to the original authors, Payette, and Champagne,[10] *"The main drawback of codevelopment is collective capacity, which prevents participants from making full use of their own abilities."* (p. 89, free translation)

A leadership group example

A pilot group of high-potential young leaders showed that the CAL approach lacked the necessary content to give them a better understanding of their role as future managers.

To develop key skills such as team management, young leaders need to have a basic knowledge of high-performing team models and how they work. To meet this need, a CAL group can be combined with complementary learning and training activities. This knowledge can come from traditional training, relevant books and articles, and coaching or mentoring from experienced leaders and/or professionals.

Also, as previously mentioned in this chapter (winning condition #6), it's important to remember that several factors can interfere with the group's success, such as competition, conflicts and incompatible authority levels.

Individual capacity

The CAL approach will be most effective when participants have the opportunity to apply what they learned to their daily work. After the session is over, does the client have the ability to implement what was discussed? Does the client feel supported in making the change(s)?

A young supervisor needs help – example

After taking part in a CAL session, a young technical supervisor felt overwhelmed by the sheer number of ideas generated by the group. "What's the best solution? How can I pick just one?"

Seeing his confusion, the facilitator helped him prioritize the ideas and create a realistic action plan. The facilitator also asked questions, to make the learning more concrete. When it was time to revisit his action plan and its results in Step 7, the facilitator scheduled a quick coaching session to help him organize his thoughts and make his presentation more effective.

Organizational culture

As previously discussed, CAL's success also depends to a large extent on the organization's culture as well as the leaders' attitude to learning and change.

Is the group operating in a culture that doesn't value collaboration or learning from each other (winning condition #4)? Are the managers or participants who say they support CAL simply paying lip service to the idea? Are managers prepared to support the new ideas and practices that are developed in the groups (winning condition #3)?

Topics

CAL sessions are based on a topic brought by a client. Are the topics presented to the group sufficiently compelling to generate learning insights for the participants? Are they perhaps too complex? Do they align with the group's overall theme? Are they overly repetitive? Too confidential? Present ethical issues or legal ramifications?

As discussed in Part 2, Step 0 provides an opportunity to answer all these questions.

The ten winning conditions checklist and actions

The purpose of this chapter is to describe the ten most important conditions for successfully implementing CAL.

As previously mentioned, if you're the person in charge of advocating for a CAL group in your organization, and if a proper needs analysis can't be done, we suggest asking yourself some key questions and gathering information from important stakeholders.

To support you in your decision as to whether or not CAL is right for your organization, we've created a checklist with troubleshooting suggestions, in italics, based on our extensive experience (see Table 12.1). These suggestions are intended to help you find solutions to the missing conditions and prioritize your actions.

Note also that, for certain winning conditions (specifically, #3, #4, #6 and #9), we give no-go situations in which CAL will clearly not succeed.

Winning condition	Definition *Troubleshooting suggestions for lacking conditions*	Check if condition is present
1. A clearly identified need	There's a clear need to implement CAL that's based on learning, collaboration, or transformation. – *Perform the needs analysis using available data: performance reviews, turnover, absence rate, 360° competency assessments, etc.* – *Get a quick needs analysis by interviewing stakeholders.*	☐
2. Alignment between the organization's strategic directions, a meaningful group theme and participant goals	The need is aligned with a strategic direction for teams and individuals: learning and development plan; change or transformation need; team development plan. – *Learn about the organizational objectives that make up the strategic plan and ensure CAL is aligned with one of them.* – *Ask executives and potential participants what their needs are.*	☐
3. Buy-in from executives and managers	Senior managers or the executive team genuinely and actively support CAL. – *Take the time to develop a business case.* – *If there's no buy-in, don't continue trying to implement CAL. Suggest another solution.*	☐

(Continued)

Winning condition	Definition *Troubleshooting suggestions for lacking conditions*	Check if condition is present
4. A learning and innovation culture	Managers and employees value organizational learning, creativity and growth. – *Recruit volunteers for the initial rollout: work with the people who want to work with you.* – *In highly competitive cultures, begin with an approach other than CAL that encourages participants to connect and stimulates collective intelligence.*	☐
5. A pilot project with measurable results	A plan is in place to measure the impact of the CAL pilot project. – *Give participants a chance to try out a single CAL session before committing to the process.* – *Clearly communicate CAL's features, its benefits and the commitment required.* – *Introductory sessions and evaluation methods should be co-created with project coordinator, the participants (condition #9) and the sponsor (condition #3).*	☐
6. Group composition	Group composition fosters open discussion and learning for each other. – *Talk to the coordinator about group composition criteria, such as appropriate participant profiles (condition #9).* – *Organize a fishbowl-style CAL discovery session to encourage people to volunteer and assist in recruitment.* – *Don't put people in conflict, competition (especially entrepreneurs) or highly hierarchical relationships in the same group.*	☐

(Continued)

Winning condition	Definition *Troubleshooting suggestions for lacking conditions*	Check if condition is present
7. A communication plan	A plan is in place to communicate with key stakeholders about all phases of the CAL initiative, including results and outcomes.	☐
	– Find the best communication channels and use more than one: email, department meeting, intranet, internal newsletter, supervisory meeting, etc.	
8. A competent and trustworthy facilitator	A competent and trustworthy facilitator has been chosen or hired to support the group	☐
	– Choose facilitators who are both competent (i.e., have experience in group dynamics, want to grow) and who have some similarities with the participants, to help build trust and understanding of confidentiality issues. See Chapter 13.	
9. Coordinated effort and logistics	Resources have been obtained to effectively coordinate the project and manage logistics.	☐
	– Suggest hiring a coordinator when multiple CAL groups are running concurrently and facilitators have other duties.	
	– Without dedicated resources, don't try and implement this approach; facilitating several groups means devoting time to this activity.	
10. Ongoing benefits assessment	Ongoing evaluations of the benefits for the organization, the teams/groups and the participants are conducted using short surveys, qualitative assessments and interviews.	☐
	– Develop evaluation metrics and tools at the very start of implementation and integrate them into the process (see Chapter 19 for metrics).	
	– Allocate resources to collect, analyse, and communicate results.	

Table 12.1 Winning conditions checklist for implementing CAL

Learning journal

In a few words, what is your key insight from this chapter?

What winning conditions should I look for if I wanted to implement a CAL group (or groups) in my organization?

If I wanted to implement CAL in my organization, who should I approach first? What resources should I be trying to obtain?

References

1. Saks, A. M., & Haccoun, R. R. (2019) *Managing performance through training and development* (8th ed.). Nelson Education Ltd.
2. Champagne, C. (2021). *Le groupe de codéveloppement: La puissance de l'intelligence collective.* Presses de l'Université du Québec.
3. Lafranchise, N. (2012). *Développement de la gestion du savoir. Guide d'accompagnement.* CSSS d'Argenteuil.
4. Senge, P. M. (2006). *The fifth discipline: The art and practice of the learning organization* (Rev. and updated). Doubleday/Currency.
5. Cameron, K. S., & Quinn, R. E. (2006). *Diagnosing and changing organizational culture: Based on the competing values framework.* Jossey-Bass.
6. Marsick, V. J., & Watkins, K. E. (2003). Demonstrating the value of an organization's learning culture: The dimensions of the learning organization questionnaire. *Advances in Developing Human Resources, 5*(2), 132–151. https://doi.org/10.1177/1523422303005002002
7. Sabourin, N., & Lefebvre, F. (2017). *Collaborer et agir: Mieux et autrement: Guide pratique pour implanter des groupes de codéveloppement professionnel.* Éditions Sabourin Lefebvre.
8. Kirkpatrick, D. L., & Kirkpatrick, J. D. (2007). *Implementing the four levels: A practical guide for effective evaluation of training programs.* Berrett-Koehler Publishers.
9. Herrero, L. (2008). *Viral change: The alternative to slow, painful and unsuccessful management of change in organisations.* Meetingminds.
10. Payette, A., & Champagne, C. (1997). *Le groupe de codéveloppement professionnel.* Presses de l'Université du Québec.

Selecting and training Codevelopment Action Learning facilitators

13

At this point, maybe you've reached the stage where you're considering whether or not to implement one or more Codevelopment Action Learning (CAL) groups. Or, you might be asking yourself what sort of facilitator you should be looking for, and how you'll go about selecting and training this person, who'll be so important to the success of your project.

Or, perhaps you're wondering whether to hire an experienced external facilitator, such as a consultant, trainer, or coach, or focus on leveraging the facilitation skills you already have, i.e., the abilities of your own employees.

The following section discusses what it takes to be a CAL facilitator, the criteria for recruiting them, and suggests ways to develop one's facilitation skills and practice.

The CAL facilitator profile

The CAL facilitator guides and enables the **co-creation** and co-learning that take place in the group. Supported by the CAL approach, facilitators help each participant **accelerate** the effectiveness of their work and **grow** their potential.

To promote the group's success, the facilitator must help create a safe space where all participants are equally committed and engaged. The resulting climate of trust encourages participants to take on the client role and openly share their goals and aspirations.

Being a CAL facilitator means showing empowering leadership[1,2] in order to make each session meaningful, and encourage each participant to learn, develop their skills, and achieve their goals as the cycle progresses. To accomplish this, empowering leaders encourage participants to talk to one another, and to the facilitator, and reflect individually and collectively during the group. They help participants practice communication skills such as listening, active questioning, and giving supportive feedback (see inserts in Part 2, Chapters 5–7).

They also create an environment where participants can feel comfortable sharing experiences, resources, and insights and encourage them to reflect on what has been shared, both during and after the sessions.[1,3–5]

DOI: 10.4324/9781032625720-17

What makes an effective CAL facilitator?

Essentially, to be an effective CAL facilitator, a person must be able to:

1. Use the CAL approach to promote co-creation and co-learning.
2. Encourage each participant in the group to ask questions and reflect in order to spark creative change and action.
3. Create a climate of trust and collaboration to build strong, meaningful connections within the group.
4. Support and guide the group during and between sessions to achieve the greatest possible benefit.

The following list presents some of the qualities of successful CAL facilitators and can be used as a checklist to select potential facilitators (see Table 13.1).

Aspects *Facilitation component*	CAL facilitator capabilities
Basic group facilitation abilities	– Knows about group dynamics and has experience facilitating groups. – Is adept at getting participants involved in establishing the group's norms. – Promotes an atmosphere of trust that's conducive to co-creation and learning from one another.
Familiarity with the CAL method	– Has experience with CAL or a similar action learning/group coaching approach. – Embodies the underlying CAL principles (see Part 1). – Knows the basics of adult learning, such as andragogy and experiential learning (an asset). – Supports and guides the group over time to achieve the goals that were initially established by the organization, the group and the participants. – Focusses on stimulating interaction, creativity, reflection, and self-awareness to promote learning, capacity development, and action. – Uses methods such as active listening, active questioning, and giving supportive feedback.

(Continued)

Empowering leadership	–	Models reflective behaviour by examining their own actions and behaviours, with an eye to continuous improvement.
	–	Provides extra resources, such as reading materials, videos, websites, etc., in response to participants' needs.
	–	Encourages reflection by guiding participants through the method, but also by conducting assessments and evaluating outcomes at the individual and group level.

Aspects *Personal component*	**Attributes of the CAL facilitator**	
Learner attitude and openness	–	Is curious, has a learner attitude, and pursues continuous improvement.
	–	Has the proven ability to facilitate in a variety of contexts.
	–	Can adjust to different communication styles and differences of opinion, which are necessary for creativity to develop. Promotes an atmosphere of trust and respect for differences.
Structured yet flexible	–	Adheres to the method's steps and guidelines, yet can adapt it where necessary.
	–	Shows flexibility in responding to the group's needs.
	–	Where necessary, feels comfortable tactfully refocussing participants.
Trustworthy and perceptive	–	Is recognized as a trusted leader by the group or within the organization, or knows how to establish their trustworthiness with a group.
	–	Uses good judgement in delicate situations, as when topics involve a conflict of interest or there's a breach of confidentiality within the group.

(Continued)

Aspects *Personal component*	Attributes of the CAL facilitator
Soft skills	– Shows empathy and openness towards others. – Stays calm in tense situations and is proactive when it comes to addressing potential conflicts.
Ethics and integrity	– Knows and speaks about CAL's intended benefits to build buy-in, but doesn't promise results. – Ensures group discussions remain confidential. Gets participants' consent for messages communicating the group's successes and other benefits to others outside the group. – Will not use the information they learn in a CAL group to their advantage. – Will not accept facilitation engagements that would place them in a conflict of interest with an organization. – Keeps their skills up to date.

Table 13.1 Capabilities of a successful CAL facilitator

Internal or external facilitator?

Deciding whether to have a CAL group led by an external facilitator or an internal resource (A "neutral" manager, or someone from HR or L&D, for instance) usually depends on the resources, capacities, and skills available in the organization, or the fit with the participants' profile and group theme(s). Table 13.2 lists the factors to consider for both options.

When to recruit...	
...an <u>external</u> CAL facilitator	...an <u>internal</u> CAL facilitator
– When there are no qualified internal resources – When the group needs a disinterested, neutral facilitator to help them deal with a potentially sensitive topic, such as possible changes in strategic direction	– When the organization has the necessary CAL facilitation skills – Where it's unlikely any internal ethical issues will come up in the groups – When a more in-depth understanding of the organization – structure, history, context, etc. – is required

Table 13.2 CAL facilitator recruitment

(Continued)

When to recruit...

...an <u>external</u> **CAL facilitator**	...an <u>internal</u> **CAL facilitator**
– To start training and coaching new internal facilitators, by co-facilitating groups	– When planning a big roll-out, as hiring many external consultants would strain the project's budget – To develop facilitation skills within the organization

Table 13.2 CAL facilitator recruitment

Becoming a CAL facilitator: A learning journey

There are a variety of ways a person who has the aforementioned qualities can acquire the skills to become a CAL facilitator, and they can be pursued simultaneously or in conjunction with one another.

The four most effective ways or methods are depicted in Figure 13.1.[6]

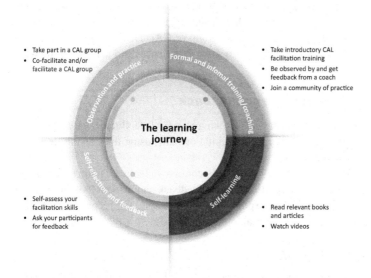

Figure 13.1 The CAL facilitator learning journey.

Observation and practice

One of the most effective ways to start building your CAL facilitation skills is to take part in a CAL group, led by an experienced facilitator. This enables you to experience the client and consultant roles first-hand, as well as observe the facilitator in action.

As part of your initial exposure to the method, we strongly encourage you to practice taking on the facilitator role by co-facilitating a group with a more experienced leader. Observation and experiential learning are two highly effective ways of developing your own facilitator style.

We recommend that your initial experiences as a facilitator be with groups that have the most winning conditions possible – see Part 3, Chapter 12. After the session, ask for feedback from the participants on your first facilitation experience, so you can continue to learn and grow as a facilitator.

Formal and informal training/coaching

Another effective way to become a CAL facilitator is to take part in an introductory training session where you can facilitate a CAL session and get feedback from a seasoned trainer/coach.

If the training also covers online CAL facilitation, that's a bonus.

You can also ask a seasoned CAL trainer/coach to watch (or listen to a recording of) at least one of the CAL sessions you led by yourself and give constructive feedback on your facilitation skills.

Creating or joining a CAL group or CAL facilitators' community of practice can also be a way to share experiences and learn from the work of other facilitators.

Self-reflection and feedback

To continue learning and growing as a CAL facilitator, we recommend that you assess your CAL facilitation skills using the Capabilities Table (see above).

We also encourage you to become a reflective facilitator by regularly asking your participants for feedback and using a journal to reflect on your facilitation experiences For example, we recommend Rosetta Pillay's reflective journal, published in 2021.[7]

Self-learning

Of course, there are many good ways of learning how to become a CAL facilitator: reading books such as this one, as well as chapters and articles on facilitating Action Learning, which is quite similar to CAL.[8–12] Although there are differences between the two approaches (see insert at the end of this chapter), you can use these materials as a source of inspiration and reflection.

In order to integrate this knowledge into your practice more quickly, we encourage you to join or create a reading circle or a community of practice where the discussion will help generate more insights into the material you're reading.

We've also provided many other references in the inserts at the end of the chapters in Part 2.

In conclusion, the best way to improve your CAL facilitation skills is to pursue a variety of different learning activities and methods. Coaching individuals and groups and regularly facilitating CAL groups is the most effective approach to fine-tuning your facilitation capabilities.

The facilitator's role

The words "facilitation" and "facilitator" are used in a variety of contexts, such as team and organizational development,[13,14] traditional Action Learning (AL) and CAL.

Foundation for the Action Learning approach

The basis for the CAL facilitator role can be found first in the three roles discussed by Revans[15] and, more recently, in those outlined by Pedler and Abbott.[8]

The aforementioned authors refer to the facilitator as an "adviser," who must fulfil three roles in the AL group, also called a "set" (see Figure 13.2).

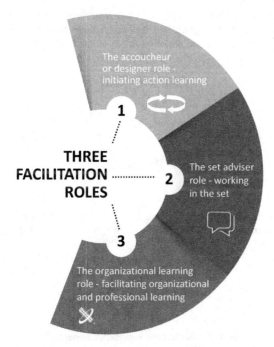

Figure 13.2 The three roles of the Action Learning adviser.[8]

The first role is that of accoucheur/designer, which corresponds to the implementation stage of AL in an organization and/or to introducing a group to the approach.

Next, the role of set adviser corresponds to the actual facilitation of AL sessions, but with the goal of making the group self-sufficient as soon as possible.

Finally, the role associated with organizational and professional learning involves building bridges between the set and the rest of the organization, either by promoting dialogue between different parties or by getting set members to talk about how AL helped them learn, or contributed to organizational change

Three aspects of the CAL facilitator role

Desjardins and Sabourin[16] focus on the role's three supportive aspects (see Figure 13.3).

The first aspect involves becoming proficient in the CAL method and corresponds to the AL roles of accoucheur/designer and set adviser. However, we should mention that, in CAL,

> the facilitator is more than just a guide or advisor. When required, the facilitator can ask questions in Step 2 to encourage discussion and reflection. They can also offer ideas and provide support in Step 4, to create even more possibilities. (p. 7)[17]

When the group has matured, and when they've become so comfortable with the CAL method that facilitation takes less attention and energy, the facilitator can play a more active role in the group.

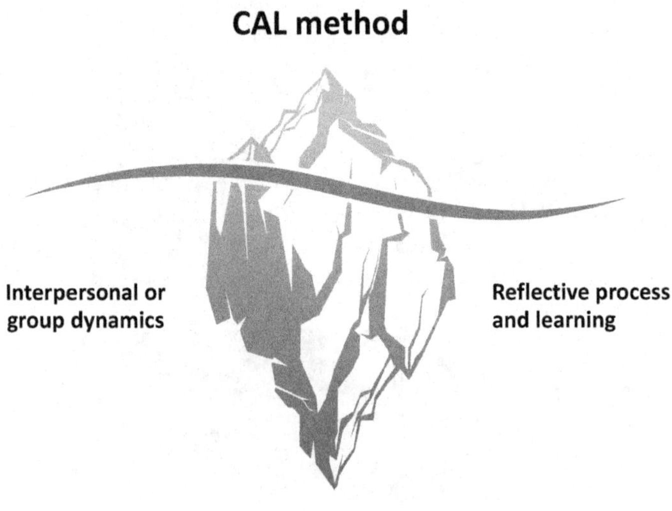

CAL method

Interpersonal or group dynamics   Reflective process and learning

Figure 13.3 The facilitator's three supportive aspects.[16]

Through their empowering leadership, the CAL facilitator actively works to stimulate the group's learning, which corresponds in part to the AL organizational/professional learning role that CAL facilitators also fulfil throughout the sessions. While CAL groups encourage their members to become facilitators so they could potentially take on this role, the goal is not to make participants so self-sufficient they no longer require facilitation, as is the case for traditional AL.

This is how Desjardins and Sabourin[16] describe the role's other two aspects:

> The method is more complex than it initially appears, because of the other two aspects the facilitator must also learn: namely, knowing how to manage the group dynamic over time, and using approaches that will enable individual and collective learning to take place. (This aspect is represented by the lower part of the iceberg.) Because CAL is an experiential learning approach, the facilitator must promote learning both through action and in action, using the concrete situations discussed in the group. The facilitator must also encourage participants to think about the implications of their own work-related practices. This involves supporting the group over time to make sure everyone gets the most out of CAL: the participants, the group, and the organization implementing the approach. (p. 296)

These three supportive aspects can be used to evaluate a CAL facilitator's abilities and their proficiency with the method. The more group facilitation experience a person has (represented by the lower part of the iceberg), the easier it will be for them to learn the CAL method. A person who feels less comfortable facilitating groups may need more training and coaching to become an effective CAL facilitator.

Learning journal

In a few words, what is your key insight from this chapter?

In your opinion, what's the best way to develop CAL facilitation skills in your organization?

Describe the qualities you think a facilitator should have in order to effect the biggest change in your situation. Why?

References

1. Lafranchise, N., & Paquet, M. (2020). Accompagner des animateurs de groupes de codéveloppement professionnel, dans des milieux de la santé au Québec, dans une visée d'optimisation du rôle. In M. Saint-Jean & V. LeBlanc (Eds.), *Formation des professionnels de santé, partenariat patient. Vers une perspective humaniste* (pp. 123–147). L'Harmattan.

2. Cheong, M., Yammarino, F. J., Dionne, S. D., Spain, S. M., & Tsai, C.-Y. (2019). A review of the effectiveness of empowering leadership. *The Leadership Quarterly, 30*(1), 34–58. https://doi.org/10.1016/j.leaqua.2018.08.005

3. Lafranchise, N., Paquet, M., Gagné, M.-J., & Cadec, K. (2019). Accompagner les animateurs pour optimiser les groupes de codéveloppement. In F. Vandercleyen, M.-J. Dumoulin, & J. Desjardins (Eds.), *Former à l'accompagnement de stagiaires par le codéveloppement professionnel: Conditions, défis et perspectives* (pp. 155–182). Presses de l'Université du Québec.

4. Amundsen, S., & Martinsen, Ø. L. (2014). Empowering leadership: Construct clarification, conceptualization, and validation of a new scale. *The Leadership Quarterly, 25*(3), 487–511.

5. Kaplan, R. E. (1996). *Forceful leadership and enabling leadership: You can do both.* Center for Creative Leadership.

6. Arnold, K. J. (2005). How to build your expertise in facilitation. In S. Schuman (Ed.), *The IAF handbook of group facilitation: Best practices from the leading organization in facilitation* (pp. 495–524). Jossey-Bass.

7. Pillay, R. (2021). *Growing through reflection: A Journal for Action Learning facilitators.* Panacea Hedging.

8. Pedler, M., & Abbott, C. (2013). *Facilitating action learning: A practitioner's guide.* Open University Press.

9. McGill, I., & Brockbank, A. (2004). *The action learning handbook: Powerful techniques for education, professional development and training.* RoutledgeFalmer.

10. Thornton, K., & Yoong, P. (2011). The role of the blended action learning facilitator: An enabler of learning and a trusted inquisitor. *Action Learning: Research and Practice, 8*(2), 129–146. https://doi.org/10.1080/14767333.2011.581021

11. Scott, D. (2019). Becoming a midwife to wisdom: A retrospective account of practice of an action learning facilitator. *Action Learning: Research and Practice, 16*(2), 151–158. https://doi.org/10.1080/14767333.2019.1611037

12. Sanyal, C. (2018). Learning, action and solutions in action learning: Investigation of facilitation practice using the concept of living theories. *Action Learning: Research and Practice, 15*(1), 3–17. https://doi.org/10.1080/14767333.2017.1364223

13. Schwarz, R. M. (2017). *The skilled facilitator: A comprehensive resource for consultants, facilitators, coaches, and trainers* (3rd ed.). Jossey-Bass.

14. Wardale, D. (2013). Towards a model of effective group facilitation. *Leadership & Organization Development Journal, 34*(2), 112–129. https://doi.org/10/gg4hcz

15. Revans, R. W. (1982). *The origins and growths of action learning.* Krieger Publishing Company.

16. Desjardins, M., & Sabourin, N. (2022). Trois pôles dans l'animation de groupe de codéveloppement. In M. Desjardins, F. Vandercleyen, & P. Meurens (Eds.), *Le groupe de codéveloppement en pratique: L'expérience des codéveloppeurs* (pp. 279–300). JFD Éditions.

17. Paquet, M., Sabourin, N., Lafranchise, N., Cheshire, R., & Pelbois, J. (2022). Codevelopment Action Learning during the pandemic – findings from two online co-learning and co-creation events: Twenty Codevelopment Action Learning sessions were held simultaneously for 148 participants from nine French-speaking countries. *Action Learning: Research and Practice, 19*(1), 19–32. https://doi.org/10.1080/14767333.2022.2026761

Using Codevelopment Action Learning to strengthen management culture and enhance leadership development

14

In partnership with Marc-André Vigeant and Geneviève Dionne, at Laval's Human Resources Department

The case of the city of Laval (Québec, Canada) illustrates a gradual rollout of CAL in a large organization.

This rollout included the ten winning conditions discussed in Chapter 12, conveniently flagged in the margin for easy reference.

The third largest city in the province of Quebec, Canada, Laval's economic growth is higher than that of the whole province. Between 2007 and 2019, its GDP increased by an average of 3.5% per year. And, in 2020, even as the entire region suffered the impacts of COVID-19, the city experienced the smallest decline in growth, a decrease of only −4.1%.[1,2]

This strong growth can be attributed to such factors as the city's ability to attract major companies, its support of entrepreneurs and the cultural diversity of its residents. Like most major urban centres, Laval's administration is changing as it looks to prepare its managers for the challenges that lie ahead. Growth and diversity mean always being ready to adopt new ways of doing things and continuously developing new skills. Accomplishing this also means providing wider access to new knowledge (**winning condition #4**).

In 2015, the city implemented a new strategic plan and, in line with its new strategy, decided to fundamentally change its management culture. It also wanted to respond to the results of an employee survey, which highlighted the need to strengthen managers' leadership capabilities.

CAL has been a major contributing factor in developing better managers and aspiring leaders.

DOI: 10.4324/9781032625720-18

Rollout and impacts

The case describes a Codevelopment Action Learning (CAL) rollout over a six-year period. At the present time, the approach continues to be implemented in a variety of ways, with a focus on continuing to move the city's organizational goals forward.

Year 1 – needs analysis and drawing up a strategy for managers' leadership development (winning condition #1)

To meet the organization's needs, the Human Resources and Organizational Development Department was tasked with drawing up managers' competency profile and implementing an effective, innovative leadership development strategy.

A committee comprising university professors, learning and development experts, and a group of internal managers was created. They worked together to review best practices in leadership development and develop a competency profile for city managers, which includes the following seven aspects:

- Team engagement
- Teamwork and collaboration
- Interpersonal relations
- Client focus
- Effectiveness and efficiency
- Creativity and innovation
- Public service and ethics

The next step was drawing up a strategy for managers' leadership development. At that point, those in charge of the rollout identified CAL as a key development tool and decided to offer it to managers on a voluntary basis. Workshops, in-class training, videos, communities of practice, one-on-one coaching, and action learning projects were also used to help develop the competencies in the managers' profiles (**winning condition #4**).

Year 2 – pilot group for senior management (winning conditions #3 and #5)

To assess whether or not CAL was a good fit, the first group involved senior management and was led by the Organizational Development Manager. This pilot group enabled the city to see how effective the approach could be. CAL groups enabled senior managers to improve their management skills in a setting that encourages action and putting skills into practice. The approach also fostered interdepartmental collaboration by enabling all participants to learn from each other and better understand their co-workers' situations.

Year 3 – eight interdepartmental CAL groups for managers (winning condition #6)

In light of the pilot project's success, the city decided to roll out inter-departmental CAL groups for other levels of managers. The groups' theme was: **Using CAL to strengthen my leadership role and management skills**. The groups' goal was to develop the in the managers' competency profiles (**winning condition #2**).

Percentage of departmental representation in CAL groups:

- *Business services: 38%*
- *Proximity services: 21%*
- *Administration: 19%*
- *Sustainable development: 16%*
- *Economic development: 6%*

However, introducing a group learning activity such as CAL was a challenge, because managers were used to more traditional in-class training methods.

In response to this, the city's General Manager and Chief Human Resources Officer offered their help in scaling up the rollout (**winning condition #3**). They appointed a project manager and developed a communication plan (**winning conditions #7 and #9**).

They also partnered with the *Association québécoise du codéveloppement professionnel* (*AQCP*). The partnership meant that two leading CAL experts and coach consultants (Nathalie Sabourin and Claude Champagne) were hired to help the project team create the right conditions for implementing the approach, as well as to lead the groups (**winning condition #8**).

Implementation steps:

- *Recruiting division heads and first-level managers*: To promote voluntary participation in the groups, managers and their immediate superiors were invited to attend a CAL demonstration led by one of the coach consultants. The demo had the desired effect: out of the city's more than 350 managers, eight groups of about eight volunteer participants were formed. This included seven new groups and the senior management group, which continued for a second year (**winning condition #6**).
- *Rolling out CAL groups*: The groups were launched, and met a total of seven times, in addition to a mid- and end-of-session review (**winning condition #10**). At the first meeting, participants were encouraged to decide on a learning goal that would guide them on their CAL journey (**winning condition #2**). At each meeting, a manager talked about a work-related challenge that was in some way related to their competency profile (**winning condition #2**). Here are some topic examples:

- Aligning teams around common goals (Engagement)
- Dealing with problematic employees and setting performance standards (Engagement/ Client focus)
- Using matrix management (Effectiveness)
- Creating team synergy and trust (Engagement)
- Mobilizing the team involved in an innovative transformation project (Creativity/Innovation)

Feedback and communication (winning conditions #3, #7 and #10)

When end-of-session evaluations were conducted, participant response was extremely positive regarding such factors as overall satisfaction, learning goals, and objective/project acceleration.

Eighty-five percent of participants took part in the evaluation, which the city considered an extremely satisfactory response rate. The results also pointed to improved employee effectiveness and efficiency, and personal observation showed stronger interpersonal relations between co-workers.

These positive findings were shared with all levels of management to persuade them to continue implementing the CAL approach (**winning condition #7**). The results of evaluations done by CAL group participants showed that they enabled managers to:

- Feel more confident in their management role, i.e., acquire more self-knowledge, become more assertive, know how to exert influence, set boundaries, make decisions
- Be better equipped to motivate their team
- Improve their understanding of the organization, leading to better interdepartmental collaboration
- Create a meaningful network of contacts and connections with people from other departments
- Take some time to reflect and reconsider their position
- Be open to new perspectives and develop the habit of asking questions rather than simply suggesting a quick fix

"CAL helped us break down silos and create real inter-departmental collaboration [...] we also developed long-term relationships with our co-workers."

"The meetings gave me time to think about what I do, and that helped me grow as a leader."

"CAL helped accelerate the process of finding solutions and solving problems."

"The support created within the group is powerful and continues, even outside the group."

Feedback from participating managers

Call for internal group facilitators (winning condition #8)

In order for the CAL groups to continue, an experienced instructor (Nathalie Sabourin) suggested that participants with strong CAL group facilitation potential be trained as future group facilitators. Her suggestion led to the city trying something new: providing each group with a manager-facilitator team. Creating a co-facilitator role made it possible to divide up the different kinds of support activities offered to participants. It also increased group facilitators' motivation and enabled them to offer each other more assistance.

In the feedback questionnaires, participants were asked to indicate their level of interest in becoming an internal CAL facilitator. Despite their extremely busy schedules, managers from a wide range of departments – customer service, IT, police, fire, libraries, procurement, HR – stepped up to take on that role.

Years 4 and 5 – eight CAL groups for managers and aspiring leaders

Following the success of the first two years, the city decided to continue the project by creating eight interdepartmental groups and broadening their scope. The General Manager and Chief Human Resources Officer continued to offer strong support for the project (**winning condition #3**).

The initial process was tweaked: two groups for aspiring leaders/possible future managers were launched. The manager groups continued to focus on improving management skills based on their competency profiles and the city's strategic plan (**winning conditions #1 and #2**). The participants' managers became more involved in the project in order to ensure their continued buy-in (**winning condition #3**) and senior management continued to receive progress reports (**winning conditions #7 and #10**).

Eleven manager-facilitators were trained by a coach consultant to facilitate their own groups. This team of committed internal facilitators decided to work together to co-create a common vision that would guide them in facilitating their group (see insert). This vision was presented to all participants when a new round of CAL groups was launched.

Internal facilitators' vision for implementing CAL groups in the city of Laval

Our purpose: We're learning together how to provide residents with better services by using CAL and helping others do likewise.
    Our experiences have led us to promote the following:

- Actively engaging managers
- Implementing a culture of innovation

- Being catalysts for change
- Pursuing organizational renewal
- Promoting personalized learning that's tailored to our situation
- Promoting action learning

CAL's success led the organizational development department to explore other action learning and peer coaching methods to enable team members to co-create solutions and learn from each other. The CoachingOurselves[3] modules were tested, and the CAL method was increasingly used in the city's in-class training so that more managers could experience the method and integrate it into their work (**winning condition #4**).

"After being in a CAL group, I felt more confident, and was able to be more assertive about my situation."
Feedback from a manager
"You learn to ask the right questions, think things through and give better advice."
Feedback from an aspiring leader

Once again, the feedback from questionnaires showed that the approach is an effective way to promote managers' leadership development (**winning condition #10**)

Topics brought to the groups by aspiring leaders included: improving interdepartmental collaboration; building a non-hierarchical interdisciplinary team; and developing your role to make a real difference.

In their end-of-session evaluations, managers mentioned the following: having a better understanding of their leadership role; feeling better equipped to communicate with their team; and being more effective at group engagement. The groups gave them a better understanding of the organization and the services it offers, which led to improved interdepartmental collaboration. Their participation also made them more open to new perspectives, strengthened their reflective practice, and clarified their development goals.

Year 6 – online CAL groups

By the sixth year, a number of changes had been introduced.

A new Learning and Competency Management team was formed to create work-related learning experiences for individual employees, teams, and the organization as a whole. The team also had the mandate to integrate learning activities, build a knowledge management culture, and oversee the overall learning experience (**winning condition #3**).

Launching this new service meant the CAL groups became opened to all levels of managers – first level, intermediate, and directors – who were quick to sign up.

Six groups were launched, facilitated by six internal manager-facilitators and three external facilitators. After five years, the senior coach consultants recommended that a new generation of facilitators be trained, who would bring a new vision to the project (**winning condition #8**).

In order to adapt to the constraints imposed by the global pandemic, the groups switched to gathering remotely. Feedback showed that the groups adapted well to the new format; although they met online, participants were still able to apply solutions to their work and their perceived self-efficacy still improved (**winning condition #10**).

Moreover, participants felt their participation in a CAL group was a positive experience that provided much-needed support during the pandemic (**winning condition #2**). However, internal facilitator-managers reported finding it difficult to maintain a strong group dynamic without any direct contact between participants.

In the coming years, the CAL project team will focus on making sure internal facilitators receive more support.

CAL's future at the city of Laval

The city of Laval's CAL groups illustrates the benefits of a gradual rollout with concrete, achievable goals that were aligned with the organization's objectives (**winning conditions #1 and #2**).

Currently, the city's vision is based on developing a five-year roadmap that will enable it to become a learning organization (**winning condition #4**). To do so, it will develop an integrated talent management strategy that focuses on sound knowledge management, collaboration, and the democratization of knowledge (**winning conditions #1 and #2**).

The six online CAL groups for city managers are still going strong. Three of the groups are led by internal manager-facilitators, supported by the Learning and Competency Management team, and three by external facilitators.

The city continues to hold regular CAL discovery sessions to help enrol new recruits. CAL sessions are also integrated in various training curriculums. These sessions show potential CAL participants how the method unfolds and give them an idea of the time required and the ways they can expect to benefit (**winning condition #6**).

Also, in order to continue building a culture of learning, the city is looking at ways to identify employees who, while they may not hold management positions, still contribute significantly to the success of the city's services and could therefore be included in the groups and might be a valuable addition to them.

Conclusion

CAL is a strategic tool to help organizations transform by developing their leadership at every level. Several Quebec municipalities, such as the city of Gatineau and the Regional County Municipality of Vaudreuil-Soulanges, have been inspired by this success and are now implementing this approach in their communities.

> The CAL groups enabled us to accelerate leadership development at the city and also develop a shared management culture. Over the years, these groups have become more than just a cornerstone of our learning activities; they have become a key motivational tool and a benchmark for interdepartmental collaboration for both managers and employees. What's more, thanks to the support provided by internal managers, they're here to stay!
>
> *Marc-André Vigeant, Former Chief Human Resources Officer; Strategist and Advocate for CAL groups at the city of Laval.*

References

1. Ville de Laval. (2019). *Rapport sur l'économie de Laval*. Ville de Laval.
2. Ville de Laval. (2020). *Rapport sur l'économie de Laval*. Ville de Laval.
3. Coaching Ourselves. (2022). *Flash Codev: Accelerate goal achievement and consolidate competencies*. https://coachingourselves. com/modules/codevelopment/

Codevelopment Action Learning rollout over ten years at the Quebec Order of Chartered Human Resource and Industrial Relations Counsellors

15

In partnership with Catherine Bédard, Former Director, Professional Development and Quality of Practice and Noémie Ferland-Dorval, Public Affairs Consultant, Quebec Order of Chartered Human Resource and Industrial Relations Counsellors

Codevelopment Action Learning's rise as a continuing education tool

Codevelopment Action Learning (CAL) was first introduced at the *Quebec Order of Chartered Human Resource and Industrial Relations Counsellors* in the early 2000s when a few groups were set up (winning condition #5). The rollout picked up speed in 2012, when the official rules for mandatory member training were put in place,[1] and again in 2018, when the Competency Guide for Certified Human Resources Professionals (CHRPs) and Certified Industrial Relations Counsellors (CIRCs) was published (**winning condition #1**).

During that period, the Order developed an innovative approach to competency development as a way of supporting CHRPs and CIRCs in developing and updating their practice, with the primary goal of protecting the public interest.

Since then, the Order has recognized a number of social learning practices, including CAL, as constituting continuing education. It felt that CAL could address some of the issues experienced by certified professionals, such as the need to connect with their peers, share practices, and engage in mutual, career-long learning (**winning condition #2**).

DOI: 10.4324/9781032625720-19

When the mandatory continuing education regulation came into effect, we recognized CAL groups as an eligible activity. From then on, we haven't stopped promoting this approach and making sure people know that, with the right conditions and procedures, it delivers top-notch results. The approach aligns nicely with the Coaching, Continuous Learning and Innovation competencies in the updated 2018 Competency Guide for CHRPs and CIRCs. In fact, our hope was that, having tried it themselves, our members would realize its value and then have it adopted in their own organizations.

Catherine Bédard, M.Ed., Former Director, Professional Development and Quality of Practice at the Order and person in charge of implementing CAL (2012–2019).

Rollout

In addition to recognizing CAL as a way to train its members, for the past decade the Order has been offering CAL groups in different contexts: inter-organizational groups organized by CHRPs, annual training for CAL facilitators, and regular articles and videos about CAL (**winning condition #7**).

Significantly, the CAL groups offered by the Order are led by experienced facilitators (winning condition #8) and focus on many topical and varied subjects, both strategic and tactical, such as talent management, leadership, and organizational development (**winning condition #2**).

CAL rollout at the Order from 2012 to 2020 in numbers

- Number of continuing education hours reported by CHRPs and CIRCs for participating in CAL groups: 4,056 hours
- Number of inter-organizational CAL groups organized by the Order: 26 groups; 187 participants
- Number of sessions to train CAL facilitators: 10 (at least one per year)
- Uploaded articles and videos about CAL: ±40

Over the years, the Order has used CAL groups as a way of connecting professionals from different regions of Quebec and from different sectors (**winning condition #6**). For example, for the past three years, HR professionals working in small and medium-sized enterprises have been helping each other and sharing their experiences. Because they often worked alone or in small teams, the CAL model gave them quick access to a support and learning network, as their peers worked for other companies, but were dealing with similar circumstances. Group members continue to connect and learn from each other, support each other, and find different solutions to their respective work-related challenges (**winning condition #2**).

The Order has decided that CAL is one of the ways its members can develop the competencies mentioned in their guide, specifically: *Organizational Development, Innovation, Coaching, and Continuous Learning*. This important decision not only makes it easier for Order members to get the training that's required by law, but also ensures that they use a structured and recognized peer training method.

> Here at the Order, we feel it's essential to provide proven resources that CHRPs can use for their ongoing professional development. The CAL groups are a preferred learning strategy for us, and a key aspect of the mandatory continuing education program. Because of that, for many years now the Order has been endorsing the approach as a collaborative learning and mutual support method for individual participants, teams and organizations.
>
> I myself have been part of a CAL group for several years now, and I really value the learning that takes place there, and the support I get from my peers.
>
> *Manon Poirier, CHRP, Executive Director of the Ordre des CRHA since 2016*

Flash Codev goes online to continue innovating during the global pandemic

In response to COVID-19, the Order recently began offering CAL groups in order to support to HR professionals through the difficult global pandemic. The groups were intended to help them rebuild their practice, be inspired by the support they received, and learn in real time through peer-to-peer shared experiences (**winning condition #1**). These newly-formed groups were offered under the title *Reconnect l Relaunch l Reinvent – Flash Codev: Six online forums*. To help professionals apply the skills they learned to their work, a total of 20 sessions were offered in six online forums, each focusing on a given sector: large companies, SMEs, public/municipal sector, HR leaders, young professionals, and coaches/consultants. More than 100 HR professionals from different companies took part in the sessions that were held online, a first for CAL.

Feedback from participants includes the following comments (**winning condition #10**):

–   *"I'm amazed at how well the approach works, even between people who scarcely know each other. It leads to a lot of critical thinking, and brings a great deal of change in a short period of time. CAL provides a framework that helps us take the time to reflect, before going into solution mode."*
–   *"CAL can be a powerful catalyst for change in our organizations."*
–   *"Our discussions were helpful because of the differences, but also the similarities between our experiences and the challenges we shared. The meetings brought new and relevant ideas, and they were also fun! They're a perfect illustration of what peer support, creativity and learning can be."*

After taking part in the forums, a number of HR professionals signed up for the new CAL groups being offered by the Order. Others got in touch with the Order to tell them about the CAL groups they were setting up in their own organizations, to help managers adapt to their post-pandemic work environment. Today, the Order is proud to continue offering CAL as a way to help certified HR professionals meet their continuing education requirement.

Note

1. CHRPs and CIRCs are required to complete 60 hours of continuing education every three years in accordance with the law entitled *Règlement sur la formation continue des conseillers en ressources humaines et en relations industrielles agréés.*

Part 4

The outcomes of
Codevelopment
Action Learning

Summary of Codevelopment Action Learning benefits 16

If you've got to this point in the book, you may be asking yourself questions, such as:

"What are the concrete benefits for organizations that launch Codevelopment Action Learning (CAL) groups?"
"What are the types of businesses, sectors or industries where CAL can be successfully implemented?"

CAL outcomes in brief

One of the most important outcomes is that participants can reach their goals faster by co-creating solutions with the other members of their group. Successfully resolving their work-related issues leads to an increase in **perceived self-efficacy** and competence, a key ingredient for performance.

Participants also develop their **professional identity** by learning more about **their own role**, their **colleagues' situations**, and their **organization's culture**. Becoming more comfortable in their role can also help a person **advance in their career**, as their increased confidence gives them access to management or executive positions. From an employer's perspective, it's also a key factor in retaining employees.

Knowing what your colleagues are going through is also a powerful catalyst for **collaboration** and helps break down silos. CAL encourages participants to build **support networks** that create trust, **reduce feelings of isolation**, and hopefully decrease work-related stress.

The whole created by the sum of these outcomes can best be expressed as: a **collaborative and learning culture** where **transformation, change management,** and **decision making** are supported by greater **trust and creativity,** leading to **new solutions.**

Bear in mind that one of the main reasons for collecting this data was to support decision making. CAL is a **low-cost**, effective solution executives and HR managers can use to develop **collaboration, cognitive,** and **soft skills** among participants, and to help the organization **innovate** and **achieve operational and strategic objectives.**

DOI: 10.4324/9781032625720-21

The CAL initiatives described in Chapters 17–19 provided us with over 2,000 participant responses. This data comes from 32 organizations, businesses, and entrepreneurs operating in a variety of sectors, including public health and higher education, the private sector, entrepreneurs, professional associations, and the non-profit sector.

The results are surprisingly consistent across all sectors – a powerful argument for CAL's relevance in a variety of circumstances and especially the **flexibility** with which it can be applied.

Finally, our most recent initiatives show that CAL is **equally effective** when implemented **remotely** as it is when used **in person**. Regardless of the format, the method is generally well received by the participants, who report **high levels of satisfaction**.

A newly hired Vice-President, Talent and Culture, at a Montreal-based IT company had two major challenges: engagement and leadership. As she watched how the company operated and how leaders led their teams, she noticed a small group of inspiring first- and second-level managers that met informally to share their issues and help each other. She saw an opportunity to spark change by providing a more formal and effective structure to co-create solutions. To do so, she used an approach that she had tried in the past: CAL.

CAL was a powerful driver to help grow our Management Team. Our CAL groups enabled Leaders to become better Leaders by learning from each other, sharing experiences and finding solutions together. They also built bridges between different areas of the company and strengthened trust between teams. Over the three years we implemented the approach, it was instrumental in enabling us to break down silos and promote more inter-departmental collaboration, which was a key business success factor for our organization. The HR Business Partners in my Team became internal facilitators for these groups, which helped them better understand the organization and enabled them to boost their impact and credibility within the company. Managers became stronger Leaders and integrated the CAL mindset to improve their team coaching skills.

Catherine Lemyre, Former VP, Talent, and Culture

CAL – a flexible, versatile approach

When there are enough winning conditions, our experience shows that CAL can be applied in many different industries and sectors and can be used by many different stakeholders, such as business owners, managers, leaders, and professionals (see Figure 16.1).

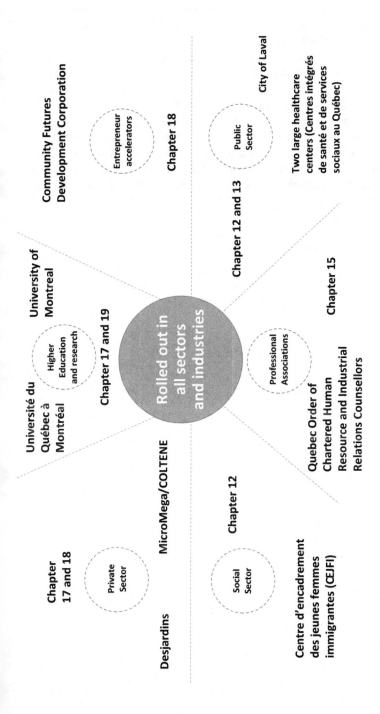

Figure 16.1 CAL's presence in all sectors.

Chapter 17 showcases two large public and private organizations that used CAL to develop their managers/leaders.

Chapter 18 discusses a group of private sector leaders as they co-create and adapt to a major transformation; a group of entrepreneurs from a variety of backgrounds who chose CAL to accelerate their business progress and develop their decision-making and managerial skills; and the story of two online forums that were used to promote social interaction during the confinement at the start of the COVID 19 pandemic.

Chapter 19 presents the results of research, conducted over a ten-year period, from over 100 CAL groups and close to 700 participants. These results can provide two-fold inspiration for your CAL initiative: first, by offering arguments in favour of implementing it, and also by giving ideas for measurable impacts you can evaluate, in order to support the groups' continued existence.

Developing leaders 17

Using Codevelopment Action Learning to build woman's executive leadership at Desjardins

Summary

This short case is about developing woman's executive leadership using Codevelopment Action Learning (CAL).

- CAL was part of a leadership development program that used this simple, effective, low-cost approach to help 100 high potential senior leaders and executives develop to their full potential. Participants were able to improve their skills in areas such as change management, team engagement, career development, stakeholder influence and self-confidence.
- Thanks to their expanded support network, CAL also helped build trust between participating leaders and gave them the courage they needed to move to the next level of management and take on new responsibilities and challenges. Before long, a number of executive leaders had advanced to vice-president levels.

Context

In recent years, Desjardins, North America's largest financial cooperative (headquartered in Lévis, Canada), has put in place a variety of different initiatives to increase the representation of women in internal management positions, among them, two women's leadership development programs. These programs are designed to enable women to strengthen their leadership abilities, expand their network and co-create solutions by learning from each other (**winning condition #1**).

Outcomes

To achieve this goal, the Desjardins Cooperative Institute, the body responsible for designing the development programs, decided to add CAL sessions to the program (**winning condition #2**).

DOI: 10.4324/9781032625720-22

Number of women leaders who took part in CAL:

- Team leaders and professionals: 70
- Executive leaders: 30

Surveys were sent to participants after each workshop, to measure the outcomes (**winning condition #10**). The program leaders also asked participants for their feedback at various times during the workshop.

Feedback from participants suggests that the CAL approach enabled them to grow and find ways to develop as leaders. CAL also helped build the kind of trust that would otherwise have been difficult to establish.

For Desjardins, the most significant measure of a training activity's success is whether or not participants would recommend it to their peers. In surveys assessing the workshops that included CAL, the average "would recommend" score was 98.5%.

The program leader said that CAL gave participants the opportunity to open up and share their leadership challenges. Most importantly, because of that sharing, they left with concrete actions and the courage to implement them. Topics brought to the CAL sessions included change management, team engagement, career development, stakeholder influence, self-confidence, and related subjects.

Comments from Desjardins' Leaders

CAL helped me break through some of the barriers I had unconsciously created for myself. Listening to the other participants gave me insight into my own preconceived opinions, and that helped me rethink my role.

Chantal Andrews, Senior Director

In an increasingly complex world, CAL has become a must in our leadership training programs as it means we can offer action learning techniques. Experience has shown us that CAL really helps leaders find concrete solutions to work-related issues, such as how to motivate their team while working from home, ways to present a project, and so on. The approach also gives them the tools to move quickly from planning to action, because of the collective intelligence and support they get from their peers.

Mélanie Montambault, Senior Advisor, and Program Manager

Developing managers over a three-year period at the Université du Québec à Montréal (UQAM)

Summary

This short case is about developing managers using CAL.

- CAL groups' focus on collaborative and cross-functional practices has helped the university's management culture evolve. They enabled over 50 managers to feel a stronger sense of belonging.
- Because they established a shared understanding of the institution's culture and its various departments, the groups were instrumental in onboarding new managers, who had to quickly get up to speed.
- By taking part in CAL, managers were able to better integrate the skills being taught with traditional training methods: change leadership and participatory management, team building and engagement, and the interpersonal skills required for management roles, such as listening, asking questions, reflecting, being open and giving feedback.
- Finally, CAL helped participants find creative solutions to many management challenges, as well as accelerating cross-functional projects because of the courage they felt after collaborating and sharing ideas.

Context

To encourage the 120 managers at the Université du Québec à Montréal (UQAM; Canada) to work together more closely, the HR director at the Vice-Rector's Office for Administration and Finance launched a number of CAL groups. In collaboration with the Association des cadres and the *Centre de perfectionnement de l'École des sciences de la gestion* (ESG UQAM; a public business school), this initiative aimed to break new ground by introducing peer-to-peer action learning and integrating it into the UQAM manager competency development program.

This program aligned with one of the four priorities of the institution's strategic plan, namely to improve efficiency by adopting a more collaborative and cross-functional approach to management. This priority was to be supported by sharing resources, enhancing managers' expertise, and creating opportunities for dialogue and mutual support between academic and administrative departments on key strategic issues. Finally, after a significant wave of retirements, faster onboarding of new managers was yet another objective the new CAL groups hoped to achieve.

Outcomes

A CAL program entitled "Improving Management Practices through Collaboration and Sharing" was rolled out for managers over a three-year period, with each year having a different theme (see Table 17.1).

	Number of groups	Number of participants	Theme/purpose
Year 1 (pilot)	2	15 *100% participation*	Interpersonal skills, such as collaboration and engagement
Year 2	3	24 *85% participation*	Operational skills, such as continuous process improvement
Year 3	4	18 *88% participation*	Cross-functional man-agement skills, such as project management

Table 17.1 UQAM's CAL rollout summary

To measure the groups' outcomes, managers were repeatedly asked for feedback, through surveys, and discussions at group wrap-up meetings.

The results of these various data collection methods led to an annual evaluation for each group, which included the following outcomes:

Year 1 (pilot)

In the first year, managers focused on improving their change leadership skills and on motivating their teams. The groups addressed themes such as: digital transformation and team development; increasing team accountability; implementing a culture of innovation; embracing change, and participatory management. Participants mentioned that their involvement in CAL groups helped them understand how other departments function. They were also able to discuss, take a step back, and reflect together on their management challenges. Finally, being part of a group of committed and caring peers helped generate ideas through collective intelligence and encouraged them to put those ideas into practice more quickly.

Year 2

In the second annual evaluation, 80% of participants said that the collaboration and sharing that took place in the CAL groups had helped them improve their management practices, which was the primary objective of launching the groups. Program organizers received many emails stating the participants' interest in joining a group for a third consecutive year.

At group wrap-up meetings, managers again mentioned that their participation in CAL helped them understand UQAM's culture, the issues the various faculties and departments have to deal with, and also helped them build meaningful, trusting relationships with their colleagues that helped them grow in their role.

The regular CAL sessions gave them the opportunity to think about their respective practices, and to collaborate in finding new and tangible solutions to problems, thereby giving them a new outlook and the courage to move forward. The meetings were also an opportunity for them to get to know each other better, which helped increase their sense of belonging and fostered a culture of mutual support.

Managers also emphasized that CAL groups helped them speed up their acquisition of the skills taught in traditional training. More specifically, the innovative ideas generated in the CAL groups were instrumental in leading managers to make changes and improvements to their teams. Finally, new managers reported that their participation enabled them to connect and share with their colleagues, and that this helped them onboard more rapidly.

These positive findings were shared with UQAM's senior managers, who decided to submit the project for the Université du Québec's award for Excellence in Management – innovation component.

In his letter of support, the then-Rector noted that the program had resulted in closer ties between managers – in fact, managers are now offering support to other teams – and increased their skills in their respective sectors. He also noted that the results of implementing CAL have exceeded the university's objectives, a prime example of which is the managers' stated desire to eliminate working in silos.

Year 3

Participants who took part in the third year of CAL – the theme of which was "Cross-functional management" – brought up the same outcomes as had been mentioned for years 1 and 2. However these cohorts specifically noted that they had strengthened the interpersonal skills that are vital for collaborative, cross-functional management: listening, asking questions, reflecting, being open, and giving feedback. They also said that they had improved their ability to manage change and given themselves permission to make mistakes. Once again, they stressed that CAL had helped them integrate the lessons they had learned during traditional training on cross-functional management.

Winning conditions

Because CAL is such an innovative approach, implementing it required the support of such senior figures as the Rector and several faculty heads (**winning condition #3**).

Receiving such high-level approval showed a willingness to break down silos – a common problem in bureaucracies. An experienced coach/facilitator was recruited to help launch and lead the groups (**winning condition #9**). She also encouraged participants to take on the role of facilitator so the university could benefit from the knowledge they acquired. This knowledge transfer created an environment of real peer-to-peer learning and encouraged managers to use CAL in their day-to-day activities (**winning condition #4**)

Managers were recruited at a CAL demo session, attended by all university managers. The two planned groups were immediately filled. The person in charge compiled the groups with care to ensure participants come from a variety of backgrounds and in order to create an atmosphere of trust that's conducive to learning (**winning condition #6**).

Comments from university managers

UQAM's CAL program gives us a way to actively assist managers in their role. It gives managers insight into the institutional culture and provides access to a dedicated group that helps them be more effective, explore innovative ways of solving problems, and gain access to a support network that's outside the traditional hierarchy. In my opinion, giving managers more ways to work together makes the university more innovative and agile.

Jean-François Champagne. Interim Vice-Rector, Human and Organizational Development and CAL participant for three years.

The CAL sessions have helped me in my day-to-day work by improving my communication, listening and collaborative skills, as well as my problem-solving abilities. The fact that my coworkers came from a variety of backgrounds and professional experiences made the thinking and talking more fruitful. Also, our discussions were very open and empathetic, and people showed a great deal of trust and generosity in sharing their experiences. I have fond memories of CAL because we learned from our peers and we also created strong and lasting bonds.

Marie-Kim Bolduc, MBA, PMP. Executive Director, Vice-Rector's Office for Administration and Finance, and CAL participant for three years.

Using Codevelopment Action Learning to accelerate business, economic, and social development

18

The MicroMega Rollout: using Codevelopment Action Learning to drive change

Case written with the contribution of Bruno Manière, Director of Praxis Management, and Codevelopment Action Learning (CAL) program initiator

Summary

This short case is about CAL as a driver of change and a way to create a collaborative culture in an executive committee

- By creating synergy among committee members, CAL helped accelerate the changes needed to achieve the company's post-merger objectives after it became part of COLTENE.
- CAL has created teamwork, support and trust in the company's new management team.
- The CAL sessions gave directors an opportunity to pause and reflect, and this helped them develop solutions to their individual and collective challenges, reach decisions collaboratively, and support one another in taking risks and initiative.
- The directors developed new skills, including interpersonal and communication skills, teamwork, reflectivity, and open-mindedness.

Context

MicroMega specializes in designing, manufacturing and marketing dental surgical instruments. In 2018, the company had to deal with a number of significant challenges arising from a unique set of circumstances. That year, COLTENE acquired the manufacturer, located in Besançon, France, and asked the existing director of operations, Stéphane Claude, to take over as Managing director. The stakes were high: he had to take on his first role as Managing director, rebuild his

DOI: 10.4324/9781032625720-23

entire executive committee, and find a way to develop and strengthen MicroMega's competitiveness within COLTENE. He quickly realized that he couldn't achieve any of this on his own. In fact, he would need to surround himself with a close-knit management team that was fully committed to the project and who could quickly get their project management skills and maturity up to speed. Furthermore, to ensure that strategic projects were implemented in a timely manner, he needed to ensure greater cross-collaboration between other levels of management.

CAL accelerates change through shared and collaborative leadership

CAL was chosen as the best approach to accelerate organizational change and lay the groundwork for the executive committee to adopt a new way of operating based on collaborative leadership and rooted in trust and unity.

The rollout itself was ground-breaking, since CAL was first implemented at the executive committee level, with participants consisting of a Managing director and eight directors. The first cycle of CAL at MicroMega lasted a year and included ten in-person sessions. Today, the approach is an integral part of the committee's management practices and has been rolled out to intermediate-level managers.

Outcomes

Based on an interview with the Managing director and a survey of the committee members conducted by our team (seven directors, RR: 88%), the CAL group had many significant benefits (see Table 18.1).

	Mean/5	Std. dev.
Action and knowledge transfer		
The CAL group helped me be more confident in my role.	4.57	0.53
CAL helped me understand my challenges and be more pro-active about finding solutions.	3.71	0.49
CAL helped me improve by interpersonal skills and become a better communicator, through listening, asking questions, giving supportive feedback, etc.	4.71	0.49
Impacts		
CAL drives company growth by developing leadership potential.	4.57	0.53
CAL helped me accelerate my projects and goals by encouraging collaboration and sharing experiences.	4.29	0.49
Collaboration and support		
CAL provided an environment where the participants could learn to trust one another.	5.00	0

(Continued)

	Mean/5	Std. dev.
The CAL group helped me understand what other participants are going through.	4.71	0.49
The CAL group helped me improve the conversations I have outside the group, when talking one-on-one with colleagues or during meetings.	4.29	0.49

Table 18.1 Survey results

In two years, the directors and their respective teams were able to manage the change journey. In 2021, they achieved the best financial results in the company's history. In the survey, executive committee members noted that CAL drove company growth by developing leadership potential (4.57/5 survey). CAL also drove change and leadership development in the committee, giving members the opportunity to focus on strategic thinking and relationships with the group.

With CAL, everything moved forward. After the merger, we worked together on building a strategy for our e-business.

We reviewed all the proposals thoroughly, with a view to the risks and benefits, and made decisions collectively. The whole process was extremely empowering, both for me and the team.

Stéphane Claude, Managing director, MicroMega

According to evaluations from the sessions, the interview and the survey, CAL enabled the company to:

– Develop ways to create a new co-leadership culture that includes shared decision-making, initiative-taking and risk-taking.
– Break down silos by fostering unity and mutual understanding (survey: 4.71/5). *"I was able to understand each person's issues and fears. The group enabled me to accept the other person's point of view."*
– Build relationships among executive committee members that enable them to undertake initiatives with more mutual trust (survey: 5/5). When faced with a problem, they all developed the habit of bringing in their colleagues, and also of offering help. *"We all have our own problems, but many problems are the same."*

- Drive change initiatives, such as building the executive committee, creating a new corporate culture, and managing a new client service (survey: 4.71/5).
- Consolidate cross-functional projects through collaboration, sharing and discussions outside the CAL group (survey: 4.29/5). *"We grow together and make faster progress when we share our experiences."*

> The members of the executive committee have come to trust one another. We're stronger as a team because we know we can tell one another anything without being judged. Working in an atmosphere of trust means we can grow faster and be much more productive. I want to carry over what I experienced in CAL to my team by developing a feeling of trust among team members.
>
> *Feedback from a director (from the survey)*

Individual committee members reported an increased ability to act confidently in their role (4.57/5) and to improve their interpersonal and communication skills (4.71/5). They also mentioned improved teamwork, an ability to step back and think through their challenges, to see issues from different perspectives, and to open up to colleagues and discuss work-related challenges. Others reported improvements in their team management skills: in delegating, taking responsibility, showing empathy and trusting others.

"Group meetings are where we have genuine, caring conversations that create a foundation for more positive relationships at work." (Survey comment)

Winning conditions

Given CAL's innovative approach, the Managing director partnered with strategy consultant Bruno Manière, who saw CAL as a means of accelerating solutions to the strategic challenges identified by the executive team (**winning conditions #1 and #2**). He encouraged the Managing director to try out the approach during one of the Proxima online forums[1] organized by his Canadian colleague, Nathalie Sabourin, during the global pandemic. The Managing director took on the client role during a CAL session. This this helped him appreciate its impact, and he immediately decided to launch a CAL program for his executive committee (**winning condition #5**). The first cycle was co-facilitated by Bruno and a member of the executive committee who was trained in CAL facilitation and coaching (**winning condition #8**).

The rollout's success was due to the following conditions:

- Have an open-minded leader who believes in shared leadership, ready to work at the same level as his team, as opposed to adopting a top-down management style. The Managing director was the first client and his participation in the pilot session helped test the receptiveness of executive committee members to the approach (**winning conditions #3 and #5**). Thereafter, each member agreed to take on the client role;
- Be supported by an experienced facilitator, as this helped everyone take ownership of the method, commit to it and be open to a sometimes-surprising approach (**winning condition #8**);
- Train an internal leader-facilitator so that the company takes full ownership of the method, adheres to the time frames, and can use it as a way to ensure new leaders learn the company culture (**winning condition #8**);
- Use CAL values as the basis for drawing up an executive committee charter (**winning condition #2**);
- Go through several CAL sessions in order to integrate the method into company processes and measure the results (**winning condition #10**).

Expanding CAL

Given the success of the first cycle, the executive committee decided to continue the sessions, with the goal of enabling everyone to continue finding solutions to their challenges (survey result: 3.71/5).

A second group, with an internal facilitator, was launched for middle managers. Nine managers volunteered and attended sessions regularly for six months. The theme of the group was: Using CAL to accelerate our projects.

Eventually, MicroMega's Managing director was inspired to offer (not impose) the program to everyone in the company. He was convinced that the skills developed during the sessions, including listening, reformulating, shifting the focus away from one's own concerns and point of view, mutual respect and building trust, would help improve working conditions and contribute to company development.

As for the executive committee members, they decided to invite CAL members from Germany, Switzerland, and Canada to attend future meetings, as a way of promoting mutual understanding and trust between members of different cultures.

The CFDC Rollout: supporting small business by helping entrepreneurs grow

Case written with the collaboration of Lucie Carignan, facilitator and head of CAL and mentoring at the CFDC

Summary

This short case highlights CAL's ability to stimulate collaborative learning across companies

- CAL has helped 68 entrepreneurs from various sectors grow by creating supportive networks of business owners.
- Participants used CAL as a way to get to know one another better and boost their self-confidence, and to generate ideas and solutions to help their businesses grow, such as better marketing, recruitment and conflict management strategies.
- Entrepreneurs strongly recommend the CAL approach as a way to learn from one other in order to improve their business practices.

Context

The goal of the Community Futures Development Corporation (CFDC) of the regional county municipality of Maskinongé, Canada is to provide support and enable the growth of businesses, entrepreneurs and projects that contribute to the economic, social, and environmental development of the community.

Part of the CFDC's support services consist of offering CAL sessions to bring together SME entrepreneurs from all sectors. The goal of the sessions is to provide them with a space to improve their business practices, accelerate their projects and create a network for sharing and mutual support.

Since 2017, a total of 68 entrepreneurs in 11 CAL groups have benefited from CFDC support. The entrepreneurs came from a variety of sectors, including: retail, food production and processing, health care, food services, hospitality, maintenance, transportation, consulting, and the social economy.

The CFDC's goal aligns seamlessly with that of the participants. When we asked the entrepreneurs what had motivated them to take part in the sessions, they said that they wanted to find creative ways of tackling issues, and to solve problems through peer-to-peer learning. Other responses included wanting to become better business owners by making connections with other entrepreneurs, and sharing real-life experiences (**winning condition #2**).

After all, business owners must often tackle the challenges posed by self-development and business development alone. However, the CFDC CAL groups provided a safe, supportive space for learning and growth (**winning condition #4**).

Outcomes

To measure the outcomes of the CAL groups, our research team sent an online survey to 42 entrepreneurs who took part in the CFDC CAL groups between 2019 and 2022. Thirteen people completed the survey, a response rate of 31%.

The survey results show that the participants achieved their objective of being more open to other points of view, thereby learning more about themselves (4.38/5), of understanding their challenges and of co-creating solutions (4.23/5) to accelerate their projects (see Table 18.2).

	Mean/5	Std. dev.
Learning and knowledge transfer		
By opening my eyes to other points of view, CAL helped me learn more about myself.	4.38	0.77
CAL helped me understand my challenges and be more pro-active about finding solutions.	4.23	0.60
The CAL group helped me be more confident in my role.	4.38	0.51
CAL drives company growth by developing leadership potential.	4.62	0.51
Collaboration and support		
CAL provided an environment where the participants could learn to trust one another.	4.62	0.65
The CAL group helped me understand what other participants are going through.	4.62	0.65
I recommend the CAL approach as a way to improve entrepreneurs' business practices by learning from one another.	4.77	0.44

Table 18.2 Survey results

Feedback from entrepreneurs (from the survey)

The groups really helped us go into detail about the other participants' circumstances. We learned about their goals, their challenges, we expanded our horizons by learning to see things from their point of view. These different experiences helped us grow in our journey and helped us see our own reality differently.

Entrepreneur, Retail food services

> It's lonely at the top! We may have teams to support us but, in the end, we're the ones who are responsible for making the critical, strategic decisions that affect our company's long-term survival. The mutual support and honest sharing among members created a real sense of community.

Entrepreneur, Retail fashion market

For example, participants reported successfully expanding their marketing through traditional and social media channels, recruiting, and training new employees despite the labour shortage, resolving internal conflicts, and significantly growing and improving their client list.

The trust that was established between CAL group participants (4.62/5) fostered a more collaborative environment, as entrepreneurs were able to put competition aside and open up to one another, to gain a better understanding of what their peers were going through (4.62/5).

Clearly, the support and resulting learnings boosted participants' confidence in their abilities (4.38/5) and in their potential to become local economic leaders (4.62/5).

Feedback from entrepreneurs (from the survey)

> This service is vital for preserving the mental health of entrepreneurs from all sectors.

Entrepreneur, Retail nutrition market

> CAL helped me find answers to some key questions: 'Should I go for it or not?' 'What's holding me back?' The group helped motivate me to take the plunge!

Entrepreneur, Agri-food sector

> In CAL, we talked about finding solutions to problems that aren't so close to home. Being more removed from the situation helped me focus on solutions.

Entrepreneur, Transportation sector

Winning conditions

CAL's success was closely linked to the qualities of the person in charge of the program and her ability to support the participants. In addition to coordinating the initiative with the participating entrepreneurs (**winning condition #9**), she was also an experienced facilitator. After having piloted CAL in person, she completed a 3-month online training program to facilitate CAL groups (**winning condition #8**).

Her knowledge of CAL and experience with the program enabled her to prepare messages that were sent out to individual entrepreneurs in the region, communicating the CFDC's offer of support (winning condition #7). She also organized talks to present the approach and established ties with other regional support organizations to recruit more people to promote CAL (**winning condition #3**).

All these initiatives helped recruit participants who were interested in the approach and were eager to participate. It's worth mentioning that, when creating the groups, the facilitator chose participants whose businesses weren't competing or in conflict of interest with one another (**winning condition #6**).

Supporting the CAL community and helping it grow

Codevelopment Action Learning during the pandemic – findings from two online co-learning and co-creation events[2]

Summary of outcomes from the CAL online events (called "Proxima")

- The two online events, held during the early phases of the 2020 lockdown, brought 148 people from nine French-speaking countries together to find creative solutions to the challenging circumstances.
- Participants were able to brainstorm ways to rethink or relaunch their business or their practice in the context of the pandemic.
- Participants came away with renewed confidence, an expanded international network, and a sense of how they could use CAL online in their consultation or related practices.

We dedicate this short case to our dear friend and colleague – Corinne Soulier – a creative, dynamic and passionate CAL facilitator who passed away during the pandemic after a long fight with cancer. Corinne, we know that you are watching from Proxima, your favourite star.

Context

In March 2020, at the start of the global lockdown, author Nathalie Sabourin was looking for a way to help leaders adapt their work to the new circumstances and bring her community together. She thought that CAL would be the best way to address this challenge.

Solutions

Shortly thereafter, Nathalie brought together the co-authors of this book to help quickly put together a team of 15 CAL facilitators from different countries. Then, two international events were held online in April and May 2020, in which a total of 148 people from nine French-speaking countries attended 20 simultaneous CAL sessions.

The events, named "Proxima," comes from Proxima Centauri, the closest star to our sun, and is a reference to the fact that the event helped participants connect and get closer during difficult pandemic times.

> The Proxima events had four main goals: (1) generate creative, collaborative and transformative spaces; (2) offer participants project-specific support and help them respond to current and/ or future challenges; (3) provide people with an opportunity to connect during the lockdown; and (4) teach people about online CAL groups through single sessions.
>
> (p. 7)[1]

Outcomes

After the event, participants were asked to complete a survey and give their level of agreement with the following statements (Figure 18.1):

– The activity helped me progress towards the goal I set when I signed up for the event.
– The activity provided opportunities to learn and gain new insights.
– The activity gave me new ideas that I will apply/transfer to my work.

Almost all participants (96%) responded positively to all three statements.

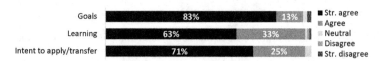

Figure 18.1 Survey results regarding goals, learning, and intent to apply/transfer.

Participants who took on the client role left the session with an action plan linked to their topic. The topics brought by the clients also helped motivate the other participants, and enabled them to become more self-reflective and self-confident.

Participants took advantage of the event to rethink or relaunch their business and/or their practice using fresh ideas generated by collective intelligence. For instance, MicroMega's Managing director decided to launch CAL in his executive committee (see the MicroMega case at the beginning of this chapter).

Because about three-quarters of the participants were CAL consultant-facilitators, they were able to come up with new facilitation resources and learn how to implement CAL in a hybrid mode, or online with their own groups.

Overall, this experience showed that CAL can be an effective way to promote creativity, collaboration and learning.

See the full article for more information on Proxima participants' achievements, lessons, and knowledge transfers.[1]

Feedback from participants

It felt great to be in the company of other CAL participants: physically apart, but emotionally close. I didn't think I would talk about my current situation – how I'm dealing with confinement – but I did and it really helped. I can never get over how effective the tool is and how, even though we're all strangers, it enables us to support one another, once the rules have been made clear.

Thank you for this session, and for your generosity toward everyone. Watching CAL groups in action, even in virtual meetings, was amazing: the participants were happy, the technology performed well, and the breakout rooms worked seamlessly. (p. 11)

Winning conditions

The lockdown highlighted the need to rethink the way we work as well as people's need for social contact (**winning condition #1**). The Proxima events were able to address both these needs.

The participants were all eager to learn and be part of a collaborative and innovative experience (**winning conditions #4 and #6**), even more so because of the constraints imposed by the lockdown.

While these factors were easy to set up and inexpensive to implement, participants mentioned the facilitators' expertise (**winning condition #8**), the top-notch organization and seamless technology (**winning condition #9**) as the main reasons for their satisfaction with the events.

Reference

1. Paquet, M., Sabourin, N., Lafranchise, N., Cheshire, R., & Pelbois, J. (2022). Codevelopment Action Learning during the pandemic – findings from two online co-learning and co-creation events: Twenty Codevelopment Action Learning sessions were held simultaneously for 148 participants from nine French-speaking countries. *Action Learning: Research and Practice, 19*(1), 19–32. https://doi.org/10.1080/14767333.2022.2026761

Notes

1. The Proxima events are described at the end of this chapter.
2. This abstract is adapted from an article published online in 2022 in the journal "Action Learning: Research and Practice," at https://doi.org/10.1080/14767333.2022.2026761

Codev-Action

19

Ten years of action research
on optimizing and measuring
the impact of Codevelopment
Action Learning

Highlights: what does the research tell us?

As shown in Figure 19.1, the results of research conducted over ten years show that Codevelopment Action Learning (CAL):

Main research findings

Self-efficacy

Teamwork

Work Politics/influence

Solutions and problem solving

For businesses, teams and groups

Social support

Co-creation of solutions
and cooperation

Transfer of takeaways to others

Knowledge about group members
and organizations

For individuals

Better knowledge of own
strengths/limits/challenges

Various human capabilities/skills

Consolidation of
professional identity

Co-creation of solutions

Figure 19.1 Main research findings.

1. Significantly improves the participants' sense of self-efficacy, generally defined as a person's belief in their ability to execute behaviours and accomplish tasks,[1] that can affect their performance at work;
2. Helps participants achieve a number of objectives, specifically: developing capabilities (grow) that are useful in their day-to-day work; developing interpersonal and communication skills (listening, asking questions, influencing others and displaying leadership); and using better resources or better work procedures;
3. Enables participants to learn about each other's work-related issues and how to solve different kinds of work-related challenges (accelerate);
4. Ensures participants get to know the other group members, which fosters collaboration and increases social support at work – essential factors for reducing the effects of work-related stress (co-create);

DOI: 10.4324/9781032625720-24

5.   Increases self-knowledge, leading to a better assessment of the participant's strengths, limitations and challenges, greater confidence in their role and a stronger sense of professional identity (grow).

Measuring CAL's impact through three action research projects

The impact was assessed by Codev-Action, a research group that was launched to undertake various funded action research projects. Two of those projects focused on in-person CAL groups, while the third looked at online CAL sessions held during the COVID-19 pandemic.

The three projects involved 33 organizations that chose to implement CAL for a minimum of one to two years between 2013 and 2021. These primarily public organizations represent the sectors of health care, education, Canadian federal and provincial government departments, and unions, among others.

Within the 16 organizations that generated usable research data:

−   64 CAL groups with 450 participants, 58 facilitators and 367 in-person sessions.
−   42 CAL groups with 241 participants, 39 facilitators and 252 online sessions.

A greater sense of self-efficacy associated with their work

The CAL format, including structured, in-session discussions, encourages participants to come up with new solutions. It also leads to action since, in Step 7, the participant-clients are held accountable for coming back to the group with their progress; see Chapter 11 for a detailed description of this step. Because the participants leave with new courses of action and the courage to implement them – both a product of the support they received – they're more likely to successfully tackle the problems, issues and/or projects that brought them to CAL.

The most compelling results, presented in Figure 19.1, include a significant improvement in participants' feelings of self-efficacy at work.[2] They also showed significant improvement in three of the self-efficacy subscales used, namely: self-efficacy in problem solving and finding solutions (an essential part of CAL), self-efficacy in teamwork, and in political skills.

Given the known impact of self-efficacy on task performance, these results are highly significant.[3] The skills learned in CAL could help leaders, for example, seek advice when making difficult decisions (political skills); become better at motivating their teams or in their own work, when they need to break down silos (teamwork); or see problems as challenges and successfully tackle them (problem solving).

Knowing CAL's impact is a huge asset for decision makers who want to build these skills in their organization or strengthen them in their role.

Improved collaboration, support, and self-confidence

Participants also reported significant improvements in cooperation, knowledge of colleagues, and perceived social support. This finding corroborates previous qualitative research findings,[4] and the following section contains more details about how much participants learned about one another. It's well known that social support in the workplace is essential for reducing, if only temporarily, the harmful effects of work-related stress. The support network provided by CAL groups is a great opportunity to get rid of silos, as many participants stayed in touch between sessions. Whether continued during work hours or after work, these new relationships can also provide people with the courage to take action, be creative and break new ground.

The same research showed that participants felt more confident in their role, improved their work-related practices and their leadership, which is further proof of the original authors' assumptions about the method. [5,6] The same was true for the participants' listening and questioning skills. [7] Given the fact that, with the exception of social support, these aspects were measured using single statements rather than validated measurement tools, future research is needed to provide further evidence of these impacts.

Methodology

Of the 450 in-person CAL participants, just over 150 completed the questionnaires sent out after each session, and also at the beginning and end of the CAL process, which lasted on average for five or six sessions. The fact that completing the questionnaires was voluntary and that the sessions were held over a one-and-a-half-year period may explain the smaller number of responses. Work self-efficacy was measured using the Raelin questionnaire,[8] which contains 30 items divided into seven subscales. Perceived social support from peers was measured using five items from the Job Content Questionnaire[9] subscale. To measure the other nine impacts, we created our own items (Table 19.1).

Impact	n	When CAL groups begin		When CAL groups end		Significant changes[a] (paired t)
		Mean/5	Std. dev.	Mean/5	Std. dev.	
General work self-efficacy	154	3.80	0.36	3.86	0.39	−2.21* ↑
Teamwork	154	3.76	0.51	3.84 ↑	0.49	−2.14* ↑
Political skills	154	3.58	0.58	3.69 ↑	0.55	−2.47* ↑
Problem solving	153	3.64	0.48	3.73 ↑	0.46	−2.79** ↑
Lessons learned	154	4.07	0.40	4.07	0.46	=
Expectations related to the role	154	3.97	0.52	4.02	0.54	=
Sensitivity	153	4.06	0.39	4.05	0.50	=
Tolerance for stress	154	3.58	0.63	3.67	0.62	=
Social support	152	4.41	0.49	4.55 ↑	0.47	−3.55** ↑
Other impacts						
Cooperation	151	3.41	0.72	3.56 ↑	0.73	−2.12* ↑
Knowledge of colleagues	151	3.40	0.71	3.56 ↑	0.72	−2.32* ↑
Greater confidence in the role and stronger professional identity	151	3.22	0.71	3.42 ↑	0.72	−3.26** ↑

(Continued)

Impact	n	When CAL groups begin		When CAL groups end		Significant changes[a] (paired t)
		Mean/5	Std. dev.	Mean/5	Std. dev.	
Listening and/or questioning skills	151	3.47	0.72	3.64 ↑	0.72	−2.57* ↑
Leadership development	151	3.05	0.75	3.21 ↑	0.83	−2.22* ↑
Cross-team collaboration	147	3.29	0.78	3.38	0.78	=
Team engagement	147	3.10	0.68	3.38	0.68	=
Team motivation	151	3.28	0.62	3.38	0.68	=
Implementing change	151	2.89	0.81	3.02	0.77	=

* $p < 0.05$; ** $p < 0.01$; paired t-tests with effect sizes from small to medium (Cohen's d).

aThe paired t-test is used to determine whether there's a significant difference between the two means being compared. Regardless of whether the statistic is positive or negative, if it's significant, there's a difference. The meaning of the statistics is impacted by whichever of the two means is taken as the starting point; in this case, the mean is when the CAL groups begin.

Table 19.1 Results about self-efficacy, social support and various other impacts

Achieving goals, learning, and transferring skills to daily life

See below for a sample of our analytical process, as applied to the goals achieved in the in-person CAL sessions.

We received 1,424 responses from in-person CAL participants. Table 19.2 and Figure 19.2 show results about goal achievement.

To what extent do you agree with the following statement?	Mean/5	Std. dev.
This session helped me make progress towards my personal goal of skills development.	4.45	0.80

Table 19.2 Goal achievement mean scores

| | | | | ■ Str. agree |
| Goal | 59% | 32% | 7% | ■ Agree
Neutral
■ Disagree
■ Str. disagre |

Figure 19.2 Goal achievement score frequencies.

More than nine out of ten participants responded positively or very positively to the question. Table 19.3 shows the main goal categories that the participants felt they had achieved.

20%	**Work-related capabilities**	*"Improve our work-related skills, find solutions to deadlocks, and share knowledge."*
19%	**Mutual assistance and support**	*"Overcome feelings of isolation, develop a sense of belonging."*
15%	**Listening, respect and openness**	*"Openness, fun, authenticity, honesty."*
11%	**Reflecting on their role**	*"Know how to fulfil my role as a social worker."*
10%	Assistance in problem solving	*"Support the client and help them find a solution."*
6%	Participation	*"Understand the situation and suggest possible ways forward."*

(Continued)

4%	Being reflective, taking time to think	*"Reflect on complex cases and some tough issues."*
4%	CAL method	*"Become familiar with Codevelopment Action Learning."*
11%	Other	*Various categories (3% or less): Workplace relationships and communication; Learning during the session; Transferring and applying skills; Innovation; Asking questions*

Table 19.3 Goal categories achieved by the participants

The participants primarily reported being able to develop their professional skills (20% of responses analysed). They also offered and received mutual assistance and support from the group (19%), and worked on developing their listening, respect and openness (15%), all of which are useful attitudes for workplace interactions. Many participants also developed a stronger sense of their professional identity (11%) and others benefited from the assistance CAL provides in problem solving (10%). The table also shows the less popular response categories. For the sake of simplicity, the next few outcome tables will only show the main response categories.

Methodology

First, for each of the outcomes (in this case, goals achieved), we first asked a multiple-choice question with an agree/disagree scale, with the goal of finding out whether participants thought they had achieved the skills development goal they had set at the beginning of the session in Step 1.

Next, to find out what kind of goals were achieved by participants who responded positively to the previous question, we asked an open-ended question: "In the CAL session you just took part in, what was your personal skills development goal?"

To differentiate between the responses received, we conducted a qualitative content analysis[10] that identifies trends in a large amount of written material and organizes them into categories that can be quickly understood and used. The analyses also helped us identify which findings are most or least represented in the data.Note that all the examples *(in italics)* that accompany the categories in this chapter are actual participant responses. Note also that the same method was used for the following sections on learning, as well as transferring and using those skills.

Learning achieved through in-person CAL sessions

Still in the context of in-person CAL sessions, we asked participants to tell us more about the different types of learning they achieved (see Table 19.4 and Figure 19.3 for mean score and frequencies).

To what extent do you agree with the following statement?	Mean/5	Std. dev.
The session helped me learn more about the topic presented by the client.	4.04	0.84
The session helped me learn more about the participants in my group.	4.04	0.72
The session helped me learn more about myself.	3.77	0.80

Table 19.4 Types of learning mean scores

Figure 19.3 Types of learning scores frequencies.

Our results indicate that the topics discussed in the group not only benefit the participants in the client role. Since more than three quarters of respondents responded positively to the question, the consultants clearly also learned from the topics; in fact, the qualitative analyses show that they did (see Table 19.5). In just over half the responses, participants reported that they had made progress in finding solutions to work-related challenges, thereby helping accelerate the achievement of their goals. These results support the fact that, when topics are aligned with the interests of the group (see Chapter 12), every participant benefits from CAL.

Participants also reported different kinds of learning about other members of their group, as shown below. Understanding one another's strengths and situation is critical to achieving co-creation and boosting team efficiency (Table 19.6).

The reflection that takes place during CAL and the resulting introspection enable participants (in our study, a little over two-thirds of them) to grow in terms of their professional identity, their role and working methods (Table 19.7). Identifying their strengths can also influence their feelings of competence; see the first part of this chapter, on self-efficacy.

Transferring and using what was learned through online CAL sessions

During the COVID-19 pandemic, we had the opportunity to work with Canadian government departments and organizations in helping them

55%	**Work-related challenges** *How to solve problems*	*"The issues my colleague had in managing the rebuilding of her team as well as follow-up issues with her senior managers."*
13%	Client's situation	*"The client was brave to share their emotions and dark thoughts so openly."*
12%	Workplace context	*"A new outreach project is being implemented in the region."*

Table 19.5 Main categories of topic-related learning

21%	**Getting to know one or more members personally**	*"Getting to know them personally, in terms of their strengths and challenges."*
21%	**Similar experiences and opinions**	*"We all want to support our teams and we tend to take on a lot of responsibility."*
18%	**Group dynamic** **Provides support**	*"Since the group was launched, the dynamic has become more supportive."*
11%	**Learning about other ways of doing things**	*"I learned about how they work, about the similarities and differences with my working methods."*
8%	Diverse experiences and opinions brought to the group	*"Participants have different ways of looking at the same situation."*

Table 19.6 Main categories of learning about other group members/participants

32%	**Reflecting on one's role**	*"Focusing on giving the power back to patients, and acknowledging my own powerlessness."*
20%	**Strengths and feelings of competence**	*"My ability to tolerate the ambiguity of our current work environment."*
11%	**How to interact with others**	*"When I act impulsively, I'm less sensitive to others. I need to learn to control my impulsive behaviour."*
10%	**Working methods**	*"I'm putting some good tips into practice that help me with time management."*
8%	Knowing and respecting their own limits	*"I tend to have high expectations for myself and set unrealistic deadlines."*

Table 19.7 Main categories of learning about themself

set up an online CAL program.[11] We distributed an online questionnaire after each session of the 42 CAL groups, that included 306 managers and professionals. A total of 241 people provided 680 responses. Respondents completed an average of five CAL sessions, out of a possible six, over a 12-month period.

In terms of learning, the results obtained from online CAL were similar to the responses from in-person participants. However, in addition to assessing the learning that was done, this research project enabled us to assess the learning that was transferred, i.e., what kind of work-related practices participants adopted after participating in CAL sessions (see Table 19.8 and Figure 19.4 for mean score and frequencies).

The majority of the responses indicate that participants used what they learned in CAL on a daily basis (85%) and applied the actions they discussed in CAL during Step 4 (75%). A majority also reported using the problem-solving (82%) and interpersonal (81%) skills developed in CAL. In terms of applied actions, participants reported transferring a total of 527 separate lessons (see Table 19.8). As shown in Table 19.9, CAL was a key contributor to better action planning (41% of responses), enabled participants to be more effective in their leadership roles (23%), and helped them discover new resources or methods to improve their performance at work (17%).

Kinds of learning transferred	*n*	Mean/5	Std. dev.
Using the lessons learned in CAL on a daily basis	654	4.06	0.70
Applying the actions discussed in CAL	656	4.00	0.85
Using problem-solving skills	654	3.99	0.70
Using interpersonal skills	654	4.01	0.74

Table 19.8 Transfer mean scores

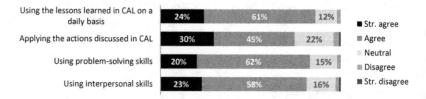

Figure 19.4 Transfer scores frequencies.

41%	**Plan to take action** (*Plan to carry out actions based on what has been learned.*)	"Give employees temporary management positions and identify skills they need to work on." "Create metrics to quantify the work generated by a given situation, such as number of requests, and the time spent responding to them."
23%	**Lead others to take action** (*Plan to carry out actions that involve other people, based on what has been learned.*)	"During team leader evaluations, as well as setting operational expectations, I will set at least one development goal for my managers." "Ask their teammates to spend some time coaching this person."
17%	**Resources** (*Implement specific resources or methods at work.*)	"Adapt the civility toolkit to the reality of online meetings." "Equip ourselves with tools – maybe a wiki? – to access targeted content."
5%	Change on a personal level (*Plan to change their attitude or how they interact with others.*)	"Improve the way I communicate with others."

Table 19.9 Transfer/use what was learned (main categories)

The birth of Codev-Action

Codev-Action is a group of representatives from universities, associations, and organizations that was founded in 2012 when researchers Nathalie Lafranchise and Maxime Paquet decided to combine their practical experience and passion for CAL to pursue two main goals.

First, their experience conducting CAL groups in the Quebec public health network helped them recognize the impact of the approach. Participants spoke of the benefits of using Payette and Champagne's method, with particular emphasis on skills development, developing and reinforcing their professional identity, and creating a support network.[4]

Given the untested outcomes initially presented by Payette and Champagne (the method's original authors)[6,12] and CAL's unproven potential to enable participants to co-create, accelerate (their projects) and grow (through learning), Codev-Action's first goal was to optimize the effectiveness of CAL and test its impact at the personal and organizational level.

In other words, how can organizations and facilitators be guided to make optimal use of CAL as a training and development approach for managers and professionals? In order to increase participant learning, Nathalie Lafranchise suggested adding a peer support and enabling leadership component to the existing facilitator role.[13–16]

Facilitator training draws on humanist values, Socratic questioning, and socio-constructivist, appreciative, and positive approaches to learning,[15,17] and has an academic, knowledge creation component. The goal of providing this training is also to offer new concrete guidelines and resources to improve the way CAL is implemented, boost facilitator skills through training and development, and enhance the benefits for participants and organizations. In fact, our work aims to increase the knowledge of everyone involved: researchers, consultants, trainers, practitioners, managers and, of course, participants.

In 2014, Nathalie Sabourin came on board, to contribute her perspective to the team's vision. She had already used her extensive practical experience and strong facilitation skills to co-write a guide on how to implement CAL in organized settings.[7] She had also played a crucial role in supporting a large number of organizations, groups, and participants brought together by CAL.

The second goal, suggested by Maxime Paquet, was to conduct a formal assessment of the personal and organizational impacts of CAL, to justify its use and improve its effectiveness. Because of their experience with a variety of public organizations, they saw many CAL groups being set up. However, as with traditional AL, there was little empirical data on CAL to guide their decisions, so managers relied heavily on consultants to help them decide when to use CAL. The goal of Codev-Action was to provide hard data to help decision makers implement CAL where it would have the greatest impact.

The results in this chapter are from three action research projects funded by the SSHRC through one Partnership Engage and two Partnership Development grants.[18–20] The projects focused on capacity building and maintenance in various organizations, and were implemented by a team of 12 researchers from seven different Canadian universities.

This type of action research requires a significant amount of time and resources, because each of the 33 organizations implemented CAL in accordance with their own specific structure and objectives. The only requirement imposed by Codev-Action was that the organizations should strictly follow the method developed by Payette and Champagne,[6] and refined by Sabourin and Lefebvre.[7]

Supporting organizations and facilitators

Given that requirement, between 2013 and 2021, all the groups were monitored and supported by a team of 23 mentors comprised of academics, graduate students, and coaching professionals from partner organizations. The support involved a variety of activities, including introductory training for facilitators, themed webinars, workshops and refresher courses, CAL groups for facilitators, individual and group coaching sessions, and any other activity considered useful, given the facilitators' background.

Despite the impact of the COVID-19 pandemic, nearly half the partner organizations (15) continued offering CAL as part of their ongoing training program.

This enabled Codev-Action to collect data from 691 participants from 450 in-person and 241 online sessions. More specifically, it collected and analysed 2,268 questionnaires from 1,588 in-person and 680 online sessions, providing a significant data pool for assessing the real impacts of CAL.

To measure the impacts, an online questionnaire was sent to participants after each CAL session. Some metrics, including work self-efficacy, were only measured at the beginning and end of the project with a questionnaire that contained more metrics.

Implications for practice

The results provide justification for choosing CAL over other training and development methods or using it in conjunction with other methods.

Evidence-based results from on-the-ground research provide concrete evidence to support and clarify the potential benefits beyond what was projected by the original authors.

The data give additional credibility to attempts at eliciting buy-in or continued support for the approach from executives, managers, or potential participants.

To evaluate the impact of your own CAL groups, we encourage you to use the evaluation method described earlier in this chapter, or use it as a guide for the metrics you wish to measure.

Research limitations and avenues

Nearly 700 participants were involved in the three research projects that looked at optimizing and measuring the impact of CAL. The goals achieved, learning, and transferring skills into practice that have been presented in this chapter are self-reported. However, they are in many ways similar to results from numerous real-life studies.

These impacts could be confirmed through personal observation or by questioning colleagues or managers of CAL participants.

The main limitation of these studies is that the conditions under which participants progressed could not be controlled, as they would be in an experimental study. However, since CAL was the only kind of formal career support or training offered to the majority of participants, it's reasonable to assume that the progress they made in their CAL group may have contributed to their skills development and, more specifically, to their sense of self-efficacy at work.

As with any other research topic, a great deal of work remains to be done. As it continues to evolve, the CAL approach would certainly benefit from further study. The existing data enables us to investigate other hitherto overlooked aspects, such as the impact CAL has on facilitators, what kinds of group support have the greatest positive effect on participants, and its organizational impact, to name but a few. Also, although our research showed that participants learning outcomes for the in-person and online sessions were similar, it would also be useful to conduct a comparative study of these two formats.

References

1. Bandura, A. (1997). *Self-efficacy: The exercise of control.* W.H. Freeman.
2. Paquet, M., Lafranchise, N., Sabourin, N., Lauzon, V., & Fazez, N. (2022). Codev-Action: Accompagnement, optimisation et retombées des groupes de codéveloppement professionnel. In M. Desjardins, F. Vandercleyen, & P. Meurens (Eds.), *Le groupe de codéveloppement en pratique: L'expérience des codéveloppeurs* (pp. 153–168). JFD Éditions.
3. Judge, T. A., Jackson, C. L., Shaw, J. C., Scott, B. A., & Rich, B. L. (2007). Self-efficacy and work-related performance: The integral role of individual differences. *Journal of Applied Psychology, 92*(1), 107–127. https://doi.org/10.1037/0021-9010.92.1.107
4. Paquet, M., & Lafranchise, N. (2014). La recherche sur les groupes de codéveloppement professionnel: Un objet en émergence. *Magazine Effectif, 17*(1), 26–27.
5. Champagne, C. (2021). *Le groupe de codéveloppement: La puissance de l'intelligence collective.* Presses de l'Université du Québec.
6. Payette, A., & Champagne, C. (1997). *Le groupe de codéveloppement professionnel.* Presses de l'Université du Québec.
7. Sabourin, N., & Lefebvre, F. (2017). *Collaborer et agir: Mieux et autrement: Guide pratique pour implanter des groupes de codéveloppement professionnel.* Éditions Sabourin Lefebvre.
8. Raelin, J. A. (2010). *The work self-efficacy inventory. Sampler set; manual; instrument; scoring guide.* Mind Garden.
9. Karasek, R., Brisson, C., Kawakami, N., Houtman, I., Bongers, P., & Amick, B. (1998). The job content questionnaire (JCQ): An instrument for internationally comparative assessments of psychosocial job characteristics. *Journal of Occupational Health Psychology, 3*(4), 322–355.

10. Miles, M. B., Huberman, A. M., & Saldaña, J. (2020). *Qualitative data analysis: A methods sourcebook* (4th ed.). Sage.
11. Desautels, C., Paquet, M., & Lafranchise, N. (2022). Groupe de codéveloppement en ligne: apprentissages et transferts réalisés. In M. Desjardins, F. Vandercleyen, & P. Meurens (Eds.), *Le groupe de codéveloppement en pratique: L'expérience des codéveloppeurs* (pp. 187–215). JFD Éditions.
12. Payette, A. (2000). Le codéveloppement: Une approche graduée. *Interactions, 4*(2), 39–59.
13. Lafranchise, N., Paquet, M., & Cadec, K. (2016). Et si on accompagnait les animateurs ? *Revue RH, 19*(2). https://ordrecrha.org/ressources/developpement-competences/2016/05/codeveloppement-professionnel-et-si-on-accompagnait-les-animateurs
14. Lafranchise, N., Paquet, M., Gagné, M.-J., & Cadec, K. (2019). Accompagner les animateurs pour optimiser les groupes de codéveloppement. In F. Vandercleyen, M.-J. Dumoulin, & J. Desjardins (Eds.), *Former à l'accompagnement de stagiaires par le codéveloppement professionnel: Conditions, défis et perspectives* (pp. 155–182). Presses de l'Université du Québec.
15. Lafranchise, N., & Paquet, M. (2020). Accompagner des animateurs de groupes de codéveloppement professionnel, dans des milieux de la santé au Québec, dans une visée d'optimisation du rôle. In M. Saint-Jean & V. LeBlanc (Eds.), *Formation des professionnels de santé, partenariat patient. Vers une perspective humaniste* (pp. 123–147). L'Harmattan.
16. Paquet, M., Lafranchise, N., Gagné, M.-J., & Cadec, K. (2017). La rétroaction. Une manière de développer une posture de leadership d'accompagnement chez des personnes animatrices de groupes de codéveloppement. In M. Saint-Jean, N. Lafranchise, C. Lepage, & L. Lafortune (Eds.), *Regards croisés sur la rétroaction et le débriefing: Accompagner, former et professionnaliser* (pp. 57–76). Presses de l'Université du Québec.
17. Paquet, M., & Lafranchise, N. (2020). Le groupe de codéveloppement professionnel: Vecteur d'apprentissage et d'efficacité personnelle par la prise en compte des émotions. In M. Saint-Jean & M. Paquet (Eds.), Émotions et compétences émotionnelles dans l'activité professionnelle et la formation (pp. 131–162). L'Harmattan.
18. Lafranchise, N., Paquet, M., Lavoie-Tremblay, M., Courcy, F., Bélisle, L., Poulin, M.-H., Kuyken, K., Rugira, J.-M., Cousin, V., Briand, M., & Hamel, L. (2022). *Démarche de recherche-action collaborative visant à approfondir l'optimisation et les impacts des groupes de codéveloppement professionnel, dans une perspective transversale des secteurs* [Research]. Université du Québec à Montréal.

19. Lafranchise, N., Paquet, M., Farmer, Y., Courcy, F., & Lavoie-Tremblay, M. (2016). *Impacts individuels et organisationnels d'une démarche d'accompagnement socioconstructiviste visant l'optimisation des groupes de codéveloppement professionnel* [Research]. Université du Québec à Montréal.

20. Paquet, M., Lafranchise, N., Gravelle, F., & Desautels, C. (2022). *COVID-19—migration en ligne et évaluation des impacts d'un programme de groupes de codéveloppement professionnel dans la fonction publique québécoise* [Research]. Université de Montréal.

Conclusion

The goal of this book is to suggest a new way of working together, called Codevelopment Action Learning, or CAL. But CAL is more than a way of working together, it's a new way of learning and engaging with others.

Even today, after many years spent researching and practicing this method, and many months writing this book, we're amazed at the power of CAL to bring people together. While the groups usually consist of people who scarcely know each other, they're united by a few common goals: wanting to improve their performance at work, help one other and, most importantly, share their expertise and learn from the other participants.

In the current context of ongoing digital, economic, environmental, and social change, the time has come to do things differently. We need to figure out how to transform the way we work by embracing innovations that will have a positive and lasting impact at both the individual and collective level.

To succeed and evolve in today's complex world and to improve today's businesses – and, indeed, society itself – we need to develop our capabilities to innovate and build trusting relationships.

We're not born with the ability to work in groups and across disciplines. When was the last time you had the opportunity to work collaboratively with others and learn from them to accelerate your goals and projects?

This book shows you that CAL groups can be started in a wide variety of sectors and industries but that, no matter what the circumstances, the groups will generally produce positive results when the approach is implemented with the right winning conditions.

CAL can help you:

– Co-create solutions to tackle your challenges
– Accelerate the achievement of goals and completion of projects
– Grow the required capabilities, both immediately and for the future

CAL is more relevant than ever: to give us momentum to move forward today and, especially, to give us the tools to build tomorrow's world … together.

What's next for CAL?

After 15 years of practicing CAL and ten years of researching it, we wondered: what's next for CAL across the globe? How can the approach reach new heights? We see five main ways for it to grow:

The learning organization, 21st-century leaders, and the skills of the future

Today's organizations increasingly require leaders, managers, and professionals to demonstrate the kind of inspirational and transformational leadership that gives meaning to their teams and empowers young leaders to reach their full potential.

With the explosion of knowledge brought about by the Internet, everyone can be an expert in their field. Yet, expertise alone is not enough. By combining our knowledge and collaborating across disciplines, we'll boost our ability to innovate and learn by doing, thereby bringing new solutions and opportunities to light.

Many influential experts – the World Economic Forum, HBR, McKinsey [1–3], and others – agree that, to get to this point, we need to find ways to build learning organizations [4–6] and the kind of human skills that allow us to co-create: teamwork, analytical skills, flexibility, or even just the ability to learn – from one another.

The same is also true for other human skills such as curiosity, openness, and creativity that create opportunities for innovation, accelerate the achievement of our goals, and provide a competitive advantage, as well as resilience that helps us grow in the face of rapid change.

Research has shown that CAL is a viable, low-cost way of achieving these goals, as proven by some 50 organizations operating in various sectors and hundreds of leaders from different backgrounds who took part in CAL groups.

Entrepreneurship and social innovation

This book also shows that CAL is the preferred solution for entrepreneurs who are looking for ways to accelerate the growth of their business and make a positive impact in their community.

Since the majority of businesses around the world are relatively small, CAL can have a significant impact on economic development. The importance of these businesses, in both developed and developing countries, is huge. Small and medium-sized enterprises (SMEs) don't just contribute to the economy; they *are* the economy!

Because these SMEs also bring communities together, their growth contributes significantly to community development and social innovation. In our view, CAL's future growth will hinge on its ongoing adoption by the entrepreneurial community.

Using CAL to bridge sectoral divides and fight global issues

Since the approach was first introduced, the vast majority of CAL groups have been launched in key industries, where CAL has been an effective tool for accelerating personal, group, and organizational growth. But what about using CAL as a way to improve society as a whole? What about introducing cross-sectoral CAL to co-create sustainable solutions for society?

Already, facilitators are thinking about using CAL as a way to bring together people from different sectors who are concerned by and determined to find solutions to social issues – such as sustainable development, for example.

As the labour shortage grows, using cross-sectoral efficiencies to address issues that affect all sectors makes more sense than ever. CAL can be a powerful collaborative tool for leaders who want to leave their silos and combine their wisdom and insights with those of other concerned stakeholders, in order to find innovative solutions and bring about meaningful social change.

Using CAL to innovate in andragogy and education

For several years now, CAL has been deployed in several colleges and universities as an innovative andragogical approach to building the key competencies of the future.[7–9]

CAL is integrated into curricula at all levels to foster innovation, critical thinking, and collaboration in action. The approach is particularly effective in internship training and can be used at all levels, undergraduate or graduate. We believe that CAL, with its principles and method, has the potential to be deployed on a larger scale, continuing to drive the evolution of education systems around the world.

To this end, our research team is currently investigating the effect of CAL on graduate student success, perseverance, and retention. The next few years will reveal the benefits of CAL for these students, who are so important to economic, professional, and societal development!

The CAL community expands

For the past ten years, the CAL approach has been growing steadily more popular in various countries, where the community of decision-makers, leaders, and practitioners who have chosen to use the approach is alive and well and continues to grow.

One example of its popularity is that corporations, unions, and professional associations have recognized CAL as a training and innovation-through-collective-intelligence tool. Other examples of its growing recognition include practitioners creating associations to train facilitators and to support and regulate facilitation practice, and the numerous papers presented at conferences and in published professional and scientific journals.

We see CAL as another, more practical application of traditional Action Learning: a version that has appealed to managers who are eager to see a return on their expectations and investment. A version that brings results, even outside the public sector.

Now that the approach is being implemented in English, the CAL community of practice has gained a considerable boost in membership. Who knows what doors will open to it now … Will you be the changemaker that lets it in?

On your marks, get set, GO! Try CAL – Now!

Our reason for writing this book was to inspire you to roll out CAL in your organization. We aim to make CAL even more accessible and expand its use around the world so that everyone, everywhere can discover a new way of working together.

This book provides you with a practical, effective, and proven approach you can use to make a real difference in your organization, accelerate change, and develop the skills of the future.

Now that you've finished the book, it's time to give CAL a try. Because the only way to really know the approach is to experience it. Hence our catchphrase: Try it; embrace it!

As with anything new, start by approaching the people who are open to new ideas. Try it, and watch as it generates insights and transforms the way people work. Each experience will be a unique opportunity to learn and grow!

Please feel free to get in touch with us and share your experiences, success stories and, most importantly, the things you learned.

Maxime Paquet, Nathalie Sabourin, Nathalie Lafranchise and Ron Cheshire

References

1. World Economic Forum. (2023). *The future of jobs report 2023*. World Economic Forum. https://www.weforum.org/reports/the-future-of-jobs-report-2023/
2. Pagani, M., & Champion, R. (2020). Intelligence artificielle: Quelles compétences pour le manager de demain? *Harvard Business Review France*. https://www.hbrfrance.fr/chroniques-experts/2020/12/32662-in telligence-artificielle-quelles-competences-pour-le-manager-de-demain/
3. Dondi, M., Klier, J., Panier, F., & Schubert, J. (2021). *Defining the skills citizens will need in the future world of work*. McKinsey & Company.
4. Senge, P. M. (2006). *The fifth discipline: The art and practice of the learning organization* (Rev. and updated). Doubleday/Currency.
5. Lainey, P., & Pelletier, K. (2016). *Devenir une organisation apprenante: un apprentissage en trois volets: individuel, en équipe et organisationnel*. JFD Éditions.

6. Marquardt, M. J. (2011). *Building the learning organization: Achieving strategic advantage through a commitment to learning* (3rd ed.). Quercus.

7. Lafranchise, N., & Paquet, M. (2022). Soutenir la persévérance d'étudiants de cycles supérieurs par le groupe de codéveloppement professionnel. In M. Desjardins, F. Vandercleyen, & P. Meurens (Eds.), *Le groupe de codéveloppement en pratique. L'expérience des codéveloppeurs* (pp. 113–121). JFD Éditions.

8. Paquet, M., Bélisle, L., & Lafranchise, N. (2018). Codéveloppement professionnel et éducation supérieure: applications académiques et soutien à l'apprentissage. *Le Codéveloppeur, 4*(2), 1–6.

9. Vandercleyen, F., L'Hostie, M., & Dumoulin, M.-J. (Eds.). (2019). *Le groupe de codéveloppement professionnel pour former à l'accompagnement des stagiaires: Conditions, enjeux et perspective.* Presses de l'Université du Québec.

References

Note: Because CAL was developed and widely implemented in French-speaking Canada and Europe, many references are in French.

Adams, M. G. (2022). *Change your questions, change your life: 10 powerful tools for life and work* (4th ed.). Berrett-Koehler Publishers.

Amundsen, S., & Martinsen, Ø. L. (2014). Empowering leadership: Construct clarification, conceptualization, and validation of a new scale. *The Leadership Quarterly, 25*(3), 487–511.

Argyris, C., Putnam, R., & Smith, D. M. (1985). *Action science* (1st ed.). Jossey-Bass.

Argyris, C., & Schön, D. A. (1974). *Theory in practice: Increasing professional effectiveness*. Jossey-Bass.

Arnaud, B., & Caruso Cahn, S. (2016). *La boîte à outils de l'intelligence collective*. Dunod.

Arnold, K. J. (2005). How to build your expertise in facilitation. In S. Schuman (Ed.), *The IAF handbook of group facilitation: Best practices from the leading organization in facilitation* (pp. 495–524). Jossey-Bass.

Austissier, D., Johnson, D. J., & Moutot, J.-M. (2018). *L'innovation managériale*. Eyrolles.

Bandura, A. (1986). *Social foundations of thought and action: A social cognitive theory*. Prentice-Hall.

Bandura, A. (1997). *Self-efficacy: The exercise of control*. W.H. Freeman.

Bandura, A. (2006). Guide for constructing self-efficacy scales. In F. Pajares & T. Urdan (Eds.), *Self-efficacy beliefs of adolescents* (pp. 307–337). Information Age Publishing.

Bungay Stanier, M. (2016). *The coaching habit: Say less, ask more & change the way you lead forever*. Box of Crayons Press.

Cameron, K. S., & Quinn, R. E. (2006). *Diagnosing and changing organizational culture: Based on the competing values framework*. Jossey-Bass.

Champagne, C. (2001). Trois pistes pour enrichir la pratique du groupe de codéveloppement. *Interactions, 5*(2), 99–110.

Champagne, C. (2021). *Le groupe de codéveloppement : La puissance de l'intelligence collective*. Presses de l'Université du Québec.

Cheong, M., Yammarino, F. J., Dionne, S. D., Spain, S. M., & Tsai, C.-Y. (2019). A review of the effectiveness of empowering leadership.

The Leadership Quarterly, 30(1), 34–58. https://doi.org/10.1016/
j.leaqua.2018.08.005

Clutterbuck, D. (2013). *Powerful questions for coaches and mentors: A
practical guide for coaches and mentors.* Wordscapes.

Coaching Ourselves. (2022). *Flash Codev: Accelerate goal achievement
and consolidate competencies.* https://coachingourselves.com/
modules/codevelopment/

Cooperrider, D. L., Whitney, D., & Stavros, J. M. (2008). *Appreciative
inquiry handbook: For leaders of change* (2nd ed.). Crown Custom.

Cooperrider, D. L., Zandee, D. P., Godwin, L. N., Avital, M., & Boland, B.
(Eds.). (2013). *Organizational generativity: The appreciative inquiry
summit and a scholarship of transformation* (1st ed.). Emerald.

Desautels, C., Paquet, M., & Lafranchise, N. (2022). Groupe de
codéveloppement en ligne: apprentissages et transferts réalisés. In
M. Desjardins, F. Vandercleyen, & P. Meurens (Eds.), *Le groupe
de codéveloppement en pratique: L'expérience des codéveloppeurs*
(pp. 187–215). JFD Éditions.

Desjardins, M., & Sabourin, N. (2022). Trois pôles dans l'animation
de groupe de codéveloppement. In M. Desjardins, F. Vandercleyen,
& P. Meurens (Eds.), *Le groupe de codéveloppement en pratique:
L'expérience des codéveloppeurs* (pp. 279–300). JFD Éditions.

Dondi, M., Klier, J., Panier, F., & Schubert, J. (2021). *Defining the skills
citizens will need in the future world of work.* McKinsey & Company.

Dweck, C. (2016). *What having a "Growth Mindset" actually means.*
Harvard Business Review. https://hbr.org/2016/01/what-having-a-gr
owth-mindset-actually-means

Gosling, J., & Mintzberg, H. (2003). The five minds of a manager.
Harvard Business Review, March/April. https://hbr.org/2003/11/
the-five-minds-of-a-manager

Gregersen, H. B. (2018a). Better Brainstorming: Focus on questions,
not answers, for breakthrough insights. *Harvard Business Review,
March/April,* 64–71.

Gregersen, H. B. (2018b). *Questions are the answer: A breakthrough
approach to your most vexing problems at work and in life.*
HarperCollins Publishers.

Guffey, M. E., Loewy, D., & Griffin, E. (2019). *Business communication:
Process & product.* Nelson Education.

Herrero, L. (2008). *Viral change: The alternative to slow, painful and
unsuccessful management of change in organisations.* Meetingminds.

Hoffner-Lesure, A., & Delaunay, D. (2011). *Le codéveloppement
professionnel et managérial l'approche qui rend acteur et développe
l'intelligence collective.* Éditions EMS, Management & société.

Jolly, P. M., Kong, D. T., & Kim, K. Y. (2021). Social support at work:
An integrative review. *Journal of Organizational Behavior, 42*(2),
229–251. https://doi.org/10/ghd3tt

Judge, T. A., Jackson, C. L., Shaw, J. C., Scott, B. A., & Rich, B. L.
(2007). Self-efficacy and work-related performance: The integral

role of individual differences. *Journal of Applied Psychology, 92*(1), 107–127. https://doi.org/10.1037/0021-9010.92.1.107

Kaplan, R. E. (1996). *Forceful leadership and enabling leadership: You can do both.* Center for Creative Leadership.

Karasek, R., Brisson, C., Kawakami, N., Houtman, I., Bongers, P., & Amick, B. (1998). The job content questionnaire (JCQ): An instrument for internationally comparative assessments of psychosocial job characteristics. *Journal of Occupational Health Psychology, 3*(4), 322–355.

Kim, K., & Lu, Z. (2019). Learning organization and organizational performance. In A. R. Örtenblad (Ed.), *The Oxford handbook of the learning organization* (pp. 332–346). Oxford University Press.

Kirkpatrick, D. L., & Kirkpatrick, J. D. (2007). *Implementing the four levels: A practical guide for effective evaluation of training programs.* Berrett-Koehler Publishers.

Knowles, M. S., Holton, E. F., & Swanson, R. A. (2015). *The adult learner: The definitive classic in adult education and human resource development* (8th ed.). Routledge.

Kolb, D. A. (2015). *Experiential learning: Experience as the source of learning and development* (2nd ed.). Pearson Education, Inc.

Kolb, A. A., & Kolb, D. A. (2013). *The Kolb learning style inventory 4.0. A comprehensive guide to the theory, psychometrics, research on validity and educational applications.* Experience Based Learning Systems.

Lafortune, L., Lepage, C., & Persechino, F. (2008). *Compétences professionnelles pour l'accompagnement d'un changement: Un référentiel.* Presses de l'Université du Québec.

Lafranchise, N. (2012). *Développement de la gestion du savoir. Guide d'accompagnement.* CSSS d'Argenteuil.

Lafranchise, N. (2013). *Étude du cheminement des groupes de codéveloppement et des personnes participantes, dans le contexte d'un CSSS.* Université du Québec à Montréal.

Lafranchise, N., & Paquet, M. (2020). Accompagner des animateurs de groupes de codéveloppement professionnel, dans des milieux de la santé au Québec, dans une visée d'optimisation du rôle. In M. Saint-Jean & V. LeBlanc (Eds.), *Formation des professionnels de santé, partenariat patient. Vers une perspective humaniste* (pp. 123–147). L'Harmattan.

Lafranchise, N., & Paquet, M. (2022). Soutenir la persévérance d'étudiants de cycles supérieurs par le groupe de codéveloppement professionnel. In M. Desjardins, F. Vandercleyen, & P. Meurens (Eds.), *Le groupe de codéveloppement en pratique. L'expérience des codéveloppeurs* (pp. 113–121). JFD Éditions.

Lafranchise, N., Paquet, M., & Cadec, K. (2016). Et si on accompagnait les animateurs ? *Revue RH, 19*(2). https://ordrecrha.org/ressources/developpement-competences/2016/05/codeveloppement-profession-nel-et-si-on-accompagnait-les-animateurs

Lafranchise, N., Paquet, M., Farmer, Y., Courcy, F., & Lavoie-Tremblay, M. (2016). *Impacts individuels et organisationnels d'une démarche d'accompagnement socioconstructiviste visant l'optimisation des groupes de codéveloppement professionnel* [Research]. Université du Québec à Montréal.

Lafranchise, N., Paquet, M., Gagné, M.-J., & Cadec, K. (2019). Accompagner les animateurs pour optimiser les groupes de codéveloppement. In F. Vandercleyen, M.-J. Dumoulin, & J. Desjardins (Eds.), *Former à l'accompagnement de stagiaires par le codéveloppement professionnel : Conditions, défis et perspectives* (pp. 155–182). Presses de l'Université du Québec.

Lafranchise, N., Paquet, M., Lavoie-Tremblay, M., Courcy, F., Bélisle, L., Poulin, M.-H., Kuyken, K., Rugira, J.-M., Cousin, V., Briand, M., & Hamel, L. (2022). *Démarche de recherche-action collaborative visant à approfondir l'optimisation et les impacts des groupes de codéveloppement professionnel, dans une perspective transversale des secteurs* [Research]. Université du Québec à Montréal.

Lainey, P., & Pelletier, K. (2016). *Devenir une organisation apprenante: un apprentissage en trois volets: individuel, en équipe et organisationnel*. JFD Éditions.

Lescarbeau, R., Payette, M., & Saint-Arnaud, Y. (2004). *Profession consultant*. Gaëtan Morin.

Lipmanowicz, H., & McCandless, K. (2013). *The surprising power of liberating structures: Simple rules to unleash a culture of innovation*. Liberating Structures Press.

Locke, E. A., & Latham, G. P. (1990). *A theory of goal setting & task performance*. Prentice Hall.

Locke, E. A., & Latham, G. P. (2002). Building a practically useful theory of goal setting and task motivation: A 35-year odyssey. *American Psychologist, 57*(9), 705–717. https://doi.org/10.1037/0003-066X.57.9.705

Marquardt, M. J. (2011). *Building the learning organization: Achieving strategic advantage through a commitment to learning* (3rd ed.). Quercus.

Marsick, V. J., & Watkins, K. E. (2003). demonstrating the value of an organization's learning culture: The dimensions of the Learning Organization Questionnaire. *Advances in Developing Human Resources, 5*(2), 132–151. https://doi.org/10.1177/1523422303005002002

McGill, I., & Beaty, L. (2001). *Action learning: A guide for professional, management & educational development* (2nd ed., rev.). Kogan Page; Stylus Pub.

McGill, I., & Brockbank, A. (2004). *The action learning handbook: Powerful techniques for education, professional development and training*. RoutledgeFalmer.

Miles, M. B., Huberman, A. M., & Saldaña, J. (2020). *Qualitative data analysis: A methods sourcebook* (4th ed.). SAGE.

Pagani, M., & Champion, R. (2020). Intelligence artificielle: Quelles compétences pour le manager de demain? *Harvard Business Review France*. https://www.hbrfrance.fr/chroniques-experts/2020/12/3266 2-intelligence-artificielle-quelles-competences-pour-le-manager-de-demain/

Paquet, M., Bélisle, L., & Lafranchise, N. (2018). Codéveloppement professionnel et éducation supérieure: applications académiques et soutien à l'apprentissage. *Le Codéveloppeur, 4*(2), 1–6.

Paquet, M., & Lafranchise, N. (2014). La recherche sur les groupes de codéveloppement professionnel: Un objet en émergence. *Magazine Effectif, 17*(1), 26–27.

Paquet, M., & Lafranchise, N. (2020). Le groupe de codéveloppement professionnel: Vecteur d'apprentissage et d'efficacité personnelle par la prise en compte des émotions. In M. Saint-Jean & M. Paquet (Eds.), Émotions et compétences émotionnelles dans l'activité professionnelle et la formation (pp. 131–162). L'Harmattan.

Paquet, M., Lafranchise, N., Gagné, M.-J., & Cadec, K. (2017). La rétroaction. Une manière de développer une posture de leadership d'accompagnement chez des personnes animatrices de groupes de codéveloppement. In M. Saint-Jean, N. Lafranchise, C. Lepage, & L. Lafortune (Eds.), Regards croisés sur la rétroaction et le débriefing: *Accompagner, former et professionnaliser* (pp. 57–76). Presses de l'Université du Québec.

Paquet, M., Lafranchise, N., Gravelle, F., & Desautels, C. (2022). *COVID-19—Migration en ligne et évaluation des impacts d'un programme de groupes de codéveloppement professionnel dans la fonction publique québécoise* [Research]. Université de Montréal.

Paquet, M., Lafranchise, N., & Sabourin, N. (2021). Des contributions d'une recherche-action pour le codéveloppement. In C. Champagne (Ed.), *Le groupe de codéveloppement. La puissance de l'intelligence collective* (pp. 228–234). Presses de l'Université du Québec.

Paquet, M., Lafranchise, N., Sabourin, N., Lauzon, V., & Fazez, N. (2022). Codev-Action: accompagnement, optimisation et retombées des groupes de codéveloppement professionnel. In M. Desjardins, F. Vandercleyen, & P. Meurens (Eds.), *Le groupe de codéveloppement en pratique: L'expérience des codéveloppeurs* (pp. 153–168). JFD Éditions.

Paquet, M., Sabourin, N., Lafranchise, N., Cheshire, R., & Pelbois, J. (2022). Codevelopment Action Learning during the pandemic – findings from two online co-learning and co-creation events: Twenty Codevelopment Action Learning sessions were held simultaneously for 148 participants from nine French-speaking countries. *Action Learning: Research and Practice, 19*(1), 19–32. https://doi.org/10.10 80/14767333.2022.2026761

Paul, M. (2016). *La démarche d'accompagnement. Repères méthodologiques et ressources théoriques*. De Boeck Supérieur.

Payette, A. (2000). Le codéveloppement: Une approche graduée. *Interactions, 4*(2), 39–59.

Payette, A. (2011). Codéveloppement et changement organisationnel. In A. Hoffner-Lesure & D. Delaunay (Eds.), *Le codéveloppement professionnel et managérial l'approche qui rend acteur et développe l'intelligence collective* (pp. 211–247). Éditions EMS, Management & société.

Payette, A., & Champagne, C. (1997). *Le groupe de codéveloppement professionnel*. Presses de l'Université du Québec.

Pedler, M., & Abbott, C. (2013). *Facilitating action learning: A practitioner's guide*. Open University Press.

Peterson, K., & Kolb, D. A. (2017). *How you learn is how you live: Using nine ways of learning to transform your life*. Berrett-Koehler Publishers, Inc.

Pillay, R. (2021). *Growing through reflection: A journal for action learning facilitators*. Panacea Hedging.

Quinn, R. E. (2015). *The positive organization: Breaking free from conventional cultures, constraints, and beliefs* (1st ed.). Berrett-Koehler Publishers, Inc.

Raelin, J. A. (2010). *The work self-efficacy inventory. Sampler set; manual; instrument; scoring guide*. Mind Garden.

Revans, R. W. (1982). *The origins and growths of action learning*. Krieger Publishing Company.

Runco, M. A. (2011). Divergent thinking. In M. A. Runco & S. R. Pritzker (Eds.), *Encyclopedia of creativity* (2nd ed., Vol. 1, pp. 400–403). Elsevier.

Runco, M. A. (2014). *Creativity: Theories and themes: Research, development, and practice* (2nd ed.). Elsevier.

Sabourin, N., & Lefebvre, F. (2017). *Collaborer et agir: Mieux et autrement: Guide pratique pour implanter des groupes de codéveloppement professionnel*. Éditions Sabourin Lefebvre.

Saks, A. M., & Haccoun, R. R. (2019). *Managing performance through training and development* (8th ed.). Nelson Education Ltd.

Sanyal, C. (2018). Learning, action and solutions in action learning: Investigation of facilitation practice using the concept of living theories. *Action Learning: Research and Practice, 15*(1), 3–17. https://doi.org/10.1080/14767333.2017.1364223

Schaeffer, N. C., & Presser, S. (2003). The science of asking questions. *Annual Review of Sociology, 29*(1), 65–88. https://doi.org/10.1146/annurev.soc.29.110702.110112

Schein, E. H. (1995). Process consultation, action research and clinical inquiry: Are they the same? *Journal of Managerial Psychology, 10*(6), 14–19. https://doi.org/10.1108/02683949510093830

Schein, E. H. (2013). *Humble inquiry: The gentle art of asking instead of telling*. Berrett-Koehler Publishers, Inc.

Schön, D. A. (2017). *The reflective practitioner: How professionals think in action*. Routledge.

Schwarz, R. M. (2017). *The skilled facilitator: A comprehensive resource for consultants, facilitators, coaches, and trainers* (3rd ed.). Jossey-Bass.

Schwarz, R. M., Davidson, A. S., Carlson, M. S., & McKinney, S. C. (2005). *The skilled facilitator fieldbook: Tips, tools, and tested methods for consultants, facilitators, managers, and coaches* (1st ed.). Jossey-Bass.

Scott, D. (2019). Becoming a midwife to wisdom: A retrospective account of practice of an action learning facilitator. *Action Learning: Research and Practice, 16*(2), 151–158. https://doi.org/10.1080/147 67333.2019.1611037

Senge, P. M. (2006). *The fifth discipline: The art and practice of the learning organization* (Rev. and updated). Doubleday/Currency.

Slade, S. (2018). *Going horizontal: Creating non-hierarchical organizations, one practice at a time* (1st ed.). Berrett-Koehler Publishers, Inc.

Tétreault, B. (2001). Une formidable expérience de formation. *Interactions, 5*(2), 53–54.

Thornton, K., & Yoong, P. (2011). The role of the blended action learning facilitator: An enabler of learning and a trusted inquisitor. *Action Learning: Research and Practice, 8*(2), 129–146. https://doi.org/ 10.1080/14767333.2011.581021

Vandercleyen, F., L'Hostie, M., & Dumoulin, M.-J. (Eds.). (2019). *Le groupe de codéveloppement professionnel pour former à l'accompagnement des stagiaires: Conditions, enjeux et perspective.* Presses de l'Université du Québec.

Ville de Laval. (2019). *Rapport sur l'économie de Laval*. Ville de Laval.

Ville de Laval. (2020). *Rapport sur l'économie de Laval*. Ville de Laval.

Vogt, E. E., Brown, J., & Isaacs, D. (2003). *The art of powerful questions: Catalyzing, insight, innovation, and action*. Whole Systems Associates; Pegasus Communications.

Wardale, D. (2013). Towards a model of effective group facilitation. *Leadership & Organization Development Journal, 34*(2), 112–129. https://doi.org/10.1108/01437731311321896

Watkins, K. E., & Marsick, V. J. (2019). Conceptualizing an organization that learns. In A. R. Örtenblad (Eds.), *The Oxford handbook of the learning organization* (pp. 50–66). Oxford University Press.

World Economic Forum. (2023). *The future of jobs report 2023*. World Economic Forum. https://www.weforum.org/reports/the-future-of-jobs-report-2023/

Appendix – Tools

CAL topic preparation worksheet – Step 0

Each CAL session focusses on an actual work-related topic, brought by the client. The topic is discussed using a structured, seven-step method that provides learning opportunities for the group.

Topic criteria:

- A goal, project, decision, or challenge
- In your area of leadership and responsibility
- Important, serious, and concerning
- Current
- A resolvable problem or an achievable project
- Concerns a situation that requires new solutions
- Encourages individual or organizational development
- A learning opportunity for the group

Subject line

The subject line will be used to announce the CAL session. Choose a punchy, concise (and possibly humorous) subject line that enables participants to quickly grasp the topic. Please ensure it doesn't reveal any confidential details about your situation.

For instance: Mission Impossible – Staying in control while managing change.

Main topic points

Summarize the most important points of the topic: why is it important to you, past actions, current actions, ideas for future actions, context (power dynamics, scope of activity, etc.) and stakeholders (i.e., the people involved, without necessarily naming them, their job titles, reporting lines, etc.).

Desired outcome

In a sentence, describe the goal you really want to pursue, such as: in the next few months, I want to get everyone on board to implement a project; I also want to resolve this issue with my partners.

Support requested from the group

Specify what kind of support you would like to receive from your colleagues: new ideas, perspectives and solutions; previous positive experiences; thought-provoking questions, etc.

How can this topic create learning insights for the group?

How do you think discussing the situation could give your colleagues an opportunity to learn and gain new insights?

Capabilities associated with the proposed topic

State the capability/skill you wish to develop by discussing the topic: team management, leadership, change management, organization, planning, etc.

Sample questions for the facilitator – Step 0

The goal of Step 0 is to help the client finish preparing their topic. Sometimes, clients can have trouble choosing their topic, or summarizing and defining the aspects of their work and/or capabilities that need to be reinforced. Before the CAL session, the facilitator helps the client take a step back from preparing the topic. The facilitator also verifies that CAL is in fact the best way to support the client, as opposed to one-on-one coaching, HR support or mentoring, and that the topic relates to the group's theme.

Below is a list of guiding questions facilitators can ask the client to help them prepare their topic:

- Why is this topic important to you?
  - On a scale of 1 to 10, how important is it for you to find new solutions?
- Looking ahead 6 to 12 months, what do you think will have changed? What do you want to change?
- In the "Main Point" section, how do you explain:
  - What you've already tried to do?
  - What's happening now?
  - What you plan to do next?
- Can you give your topic a short title that would fit into a 280-character "tweet", for instance?
- What do you hope to achieve through the CAL session?
  - What are your hopes and fears for the upcoming session?
- Are there any potential confidentiality, ethics or other sensitive issues? Are any participants involved or impacted by this topic?
- How does your topic align with the group's theme?
- Will this topic be as a learning experience for your fellow participants? How?
- What leadership capabilities do you need to achieve your objective?
- As the facilitator, what can I do to support you during the session?
- Do you want to share or check anything else before the session starts (CAL method, concerns, questions, etc.)?
- How do you want your topic to be presented in the group email?
- What are you taking away from our discussion? What value did we create together?

Information to be shared by the facilitator:

- The client should fill out the preparation worksheet and email it to the facilitator before the session.

The client can bring copies of this sheet and hand them out to all the group members (or to share on the screen for an online session). We do not recommend to send the preparation sheet by email.

CAL think sheet – Seven steps

1. PARTICIPANT GOALS AND TOPIC

My learning intention/goal for this session (≈ 10 min)

Options: (1) gain a deeper understanding of the topic; (2) develop skills related to the CAL method (active listening, asking questions, giving feedback, reflective practice; (3) learn more about the CAL method; (4) depending on the theme, acquire a new skill or competency

Presentation of the topic by the client (≈ 10 min)

2. ASKING QUESTIONS (≈ 20 min)

See "Sample powerful questions guide – step 2"

3. REFRAMING (≈ 15 min)

Reframing by the consultants: I understand... I hear... I feel... I wonder...

Reframing by the client: My goal is...I need support from the group...

4.   IDEATION, REFLECTION AND SUPPORT ($\approx$ 20 min)

5.   INSIGHTS AND ACTION PLAN ($\approx$ 10 min)

6.   TAKEAWAYS ANS APPLICATIONS ($\approx$ 20 min)
Acquired learning & Takeaways: What I learned about the topic?; What I learned about myself or my abilities; What I learned about the group? *Actions: Actions I will integrate into my daily routine; New methods I will try at work; Things I will do differently* *Assessment: What inspired me; What I especially liked and/or was surprised by; What I would like the group to do differently?* *Intents/goals: How I feel about achieving my learning intention and/or goal?*

7.   FOLLOW UP AND ACCOUNTABILITY ($\approx$ 15 min)
Since the last CAL session, my insights and key take-away are?

Sample powerful questions guide – Step 2

In a CAL group, you are encouraged to ask questions that focus on three areas of interest: the topic itself; the context; and the client's actions, thoughts, and emotional experiences.

The topic

- Who is involved? Who are the stakeholders?
- What is going well?
- What has already been done or implemented? What are the solutions you have considered?
- How? / Where? /When?
- What are the impacts or effects?
- What options do you have? Which is the riskiest, the most innovative, the safest?
- What is the risk of doing nothing?
- What challenges are you facing? What challenges could arise?
- Do you see a way of resolving this issue? What requires immediate attention from us to allow you to move forward?
- What conversation could we have today that would have a broad effect and create new possibilities for the outcome of your situation?
- What question would change the outcome of your situation the most?
- What do we know so far and what do we still have to learn about your situation?
- If success was guaranteed, what radical action could you take?
- Is this situation recurrent? (Frequency)

The context

- What are the obstacles and hurdles around you?
- Who are your allies, your opponents?
- Tell me about your organization's culture.
- What are the levels of power of the various actors?
- What is the organizational structure's impact on your situation?
- What would be the impact of the status quo?
- What are the existing rules and standards?
- How can you relate the issue to the current context/circumstances?
- What is the decision-making process?
- What is the communication style within the organization?

– What could happen to help you feel completely committed to, and energized by, your situation?
– What can be done and for whom is it important? (Rather than "What isn't working and who is responsible?")
– What would trigger a change in the way this situation is perceived?

The client
– What concerns you genuinely? How is this important to you?
– What is your intent? Your key objective?
– What risks are you ready to take to succeed?
– What strengths will you use to succeed?
– What do you have control over? What is out of your control?
– What is your reaction to this situation? How do you experience this?
– How does this situation speak to your own values?
– What are your expectations and those of your boss?
– What are your needs?
– What makes you hesitate? What do you fear?
– If you were in someone else's shoes...
– What are your weaknesses?
– In relation to this situation: What is your energy level? What is your motivation? What is your timeline?
– What is the most important thing you have learned, understood or discovered up until now?
– What do you take away from the different opinions presented?

Step 7 preparation worksheet

The goal of the CAL approach is to use reflection and sharing to consolidate the participants' work practice and give them the courage to implement new courses of action. In the upcoming session, we encourage you to share the progress you made in implementing your action plan, the questions you asked yourself, and the lessons you learned. This kind of sharing also benefits your colleagues as it enables them to learn as you learn, together.

At the last session, my expected result was:

My action plan was:

What I did since the last sessions and the most significant impact:

Results, success, move in the wrong direction or reversal/disappointment/questioning...

What I have left to do and the resources I will use to get there:

My reflections and lessons learned are:

State the lessons you learned with respect to your learning intentions/session goals and/or your initial reasons for joining a CAL group, your current concerns, your feelings, your commitment to move forward to resolve your issue and/or solve your problem, etc.

CAL participation form

My CAL group theme

My learning intention/goal for the whole CAL cycle
Examples: (1) develop skills related to the CAL method (active listening, asking questions, giving feedback, reflective practice; (2) learn more about the CAL method; (3) depending on the groups' theme, acquire a new skill or competency.

CAL's three main guiding principles – My commitment

In order to foster a safe learning environment, I agree to follow and abide by the following guiding principles:

1. **Be committed to the group.** This is voluntary and stems from each participant's personal sense of responsibility.

2. **Be collaborative and supportive.** This is based on an attitude of mutual goodwill, openness and trust.

3. **Be respectful and discrete.** This applies to all personal, confidential details discussed in the group.

   Add other principles if required (ex.: online).

Participant's signature:	Date:

Manager's commitment (*if required*)
I agree to support the participant as they actively participate in CAL and work towards achieving their learning intention/goal.

Manager's signature:	Date:

Index

Note: **Bold** page numbers refer to tables and *italic* page numbers refer to figures.

Printed in the United States
by Baker & Taylor Publisher Services